worlds
of wonder

How to Write Science Fiction

& Fantasy

worlds of wonder

How to Write Science Fiction
& Fantasy

David Gerrold

WRITER'S DIGEST BOOKS
CINCINNATI, OH
www.writersdigest.com

Visit our Web site at www.writersdigest.com for information on more resources for writers.

To receive a free weekly e-mail newsletter delivering tips and updates about
writing and about Writer's Digest products, send an e-mail with "Subscribe
Newsletter" in the body of the message to newsletter-request@writersdigest.c
om, or register directly at our Web site at www.writersdigest.com.

05   04   03   02   01   5   4   3   2   1

Library of Congress Cataloging-in-Publication Data

Gerrold, David
    Worlds of wonder: how to write science fiction and fantasy / by Gerrold,
    David.—1st ed.
        p.   cm.
    Includes index.
    ISBN 1-58297-007-6 (pbk.)
        1. Science fiction—Authorship. I. Title.

PN3377.5.S3 647   2001
808.3/8762—dc21   00-051299
                                                          CIP

Edited by David Borcherding and Michelle Howry
Interior designed by Angela Wilcox
Cover designed by Wendy Dunning
Cover photography by Digital Imagery © copyright 2000 Photo Disc, Inc.
Production coordinated by Mark Griffin

For my students.

Thank you for all you have taught me.

About the Author

David Gerrold was raised in the San Fernando Valley by Ward and June Cleaver. Nobody in his family was alcoholic, abusive, addicted, or otherwise dysfunctional. This lack of serious childhood trauma nearly destroyed Gerrold's budding ability as a writer. He had no source material. Nevertheless, through constant and deliberate self-exposure to comic books, science fiction pulp magazines, and trashy B-movies, the young Gerrold was able to sink to the necessary level of moral dissolution to become a successful author.

In 1967, Gerrold became the youngest ever member of the Writers Guild of America when he sold his first television script, "The Trouble With Tribbles" episode of *Star Trek*. The episode was nominated for the prestigious Hugo Award. Paramount Pictures identifies "The Trouble With Tribbles" as the single most popular episode of all *Star Trek* episodes.

From 1972 to 1973, David Gerrold published nine books: two nonfiction books about *Star Trek*, an anthology, a short story collection, and five novels. The novels were *Yesterday's Children* (the first Star Wolf novel), *When Harlie Was One* (1972 Hugo and Nebula award nominee), *The Man Who Folded Himself* (1973 Hugo and Nebula award nominee), *Space Skimmer* (one of his most reprinted novels), and the novelization of *Battle For The Planet Of The Apes*. (Gerrold can be seen as a dead ape in one of the movie's climactic scenes.)

For a while, during the seventies, Gerrold lived in Ireland and then New York. When he returned to Los Angeles, he resumed working in television. He created *Land of the Lost* for Sid and Marty Krofft, and served as story-editor/producer for the first season, writing five episodes. He also wrote episodes for *Star Trek Animated, Logan's Run, Tales From The Darkside, Twilight Zone, The Real Ghost Busters, Superboy,* and *Babylon 5.* He served as a story-editor/producer for the first season of *Star Trek: The Next Generation.*

At the beginning of the eighties, Gerrold began teaching screenwriting at Pepperdine University in Malibu. Although his students call him "The Teacher From The Black Lagoon," they also rank him as one of the most effective instructors on campus. Gerrold also conducts an infrequent seminar on authorship called "Writing On Purpose."

In 1984, Gerrold published *A Matter For Men*, the first novel in his epic series of alien invasion, *The War Against The Chtorr.* In 1985, the second novel appeared, *A Day For Damnation.* The series has developed an enthusiastic cult following. *A Rage For Revenge* and *A Season For Slaughter* were published in 1989 and 1993. A fifth book, *A Method For Madness*, is due Real Soon Now.

Gerrold's other books include *Moonstar Odyssey, Enemy Mine* (a novelization), *Chess With A Dragon, The Voyage of the Star Wolf, The Middle of Nowhere, Under The Eye of God, A Covenant of Justice,* and *Fatal Distractions.* The latter effort is a history of shareware computer games, with an accompanying CD-ROM of software.

Gerrold's novellette, *The Martian Child*, was published in the September, 1994, issue of *The Magazine of Fantasy & Science Fiction.* In 1995, it won the Nebula for best novelette of the year. Two months later, the story won the Locus Readership Poll, and two months after that the Hugo award, completing a rare sweep of science fiction's "triple crown."

David and and his son Sean live in California with three neurotic dogs and an assortment of spoiled cats.

Table of Contents

Start Here

Every great writer was once a beginner.
Remember that. Don't beat yourself up for not
knowing something. Go out and learn it.

The very best writing instructor I ever had was an incompetent.

A terminal alcoholic who could barely find the classroom each day, he was a bleary-eyed, red-nosed, overstuffed, walking elbow-wrinkle of a human being. Whatever writing ability he'd ever had, he'd long-since drowned it, and the corpse was a layer of dried sediment at the bottom of a bottle.

He didn't like me either.

His lectures were a waste of time. His assignments were pointless. The class was as challenging as the hole in a doughnut. Custard had more substance.

But one day he said to me *the most important words in my entire career*. Had he not said these words, my life would have been far different—I probably would not have become a writer. He looked me straight in the eye and said, "Stop wasting my time. *You're no good. You'll never be any good. You have no talent. You'll never be a writer.*"

His words angered me so much that I made a promise to myself. It was very simple. *I'll show you, you stupid old bastard!*

That was in 1963.

Within four years I'd sold a script to television—"The Trouble With Tribbles" episode of *Star Trek*. Within ten years I'd published eight novels, two anthologies, two nonfiction books about television production, and a short story collection. I'd written four more television scripts. And I'd won three Hugo and three Nebula nominations.

Boy, I showed him.

And yes, rage is an excellent fuel.

Later on, when the rage faded out, I discovered that rage isn't enough. A writer also needs technique. And that's why he was an incompetent instructor, because he failed to teach the necessary skills for carrying a narrative over the inevitable rough spots—he failed to teach *technique*.

The second-best writing instructor I ever had was Irwin R. Blacker at USC Film School. Blacker's theory of writing could be summed up in three words: "Structure! Structure! Structure!"

That was the beginning. Those three words opened the door to understanding. From that moment, storytelling as a craft ceased to be a mystery and began to be an adventure. I wondered what other *secrets* I could discover.

The trick was to learn from *real* writers.

A few years later, I started to attend science fiction conventions. The most exciting moments occurred when some of the best writers and editors in the field appeared on panels and spoke candidly of their own discoveries and insights: Harlan Ellison, Frederik Pohl, Anne McCaffrey, Isaac Asimov, Theodore Sturgeon, James Blish, Robert Silverberg, Terry Carr, Randall Garrett, Harry Harrison, and many others whose work I admired.

As a beginner, I was envious of the mastery that the pros in the field took for granted. I wondered how they had gained such wisdom and despaired that I would ever achieve that same kind of skill. At the beginning, every sentence was an effort, every paragraph was an obstacle, every chapter completed was a victory. Writing was *hard*.

(And it never gets any easier. It just gets harder in different ways.)

Here's the paradox:

There's a lot of technique to learn, and you can only learn it by doing. Writing teaches itself in the act of writing—but only *after* you learn the technique, do you find out that writing well is *not* about technique at all.

There is another domain of creativity, another way of being, a process *beyond* mere technique. I had inadvertently stumbled into it when I used rage as my fuel, but I hadn't realized at the time what I'd learned. Only much later did I start to recognize the questions I should have been asking:

- How do I take the reader someplace else and make him glad he went?
- How do I create an experience of another life so vivid and compelling that for the moment it exists in the mind, it obscures and obliterates the experience of the reader's own life?
- How do I transport human consciousness into the realm of exhilaration and transformation?
- How can I get so deeply into my story that I am telling it from the inside?

The first time I asked these questions, they looked unanswerable. That was because I still thought that writing had to be *important*. That was my mistake. Writing is not important by itself. It is only important if it makes a difference. (Yes, it's fun to be important—but it's more important to have fun.)

The truth is that storytelling is a natural skill—it's part of being human. It's how our intelligence manifests itself—through conceptualization. Every human being does it. Almost everything we say is a story.

When you tell a joke, you're telling a story. When you tell a lie, you're telling a different kind of story. When you explain why you were late getting home, or what happened to the chocolate cake, or why the dog is wearing your sister's hat, you're telling a story. Every time you relate an experience, you are automatically shifting into storytelling mode. The listener meets you halfway, because he wants to hear about the *discovery* that is at the heart of every story.

This is the essential definition of a story:

A person has a problem, he explores the problem until he understands it, finally he makes a choice (usually a difficult one) that produces a transformation of understanding and resolves the difficulty. So a story is about the experience of problem solving and the lessons learned.

This is the insight:

Storytelling is the essential expression of human consciousness. It is the way the mind conceptualizes and stores experiences; the mind relates to the universe as things to be discovered, understood, and mastered: *problems*. We see things as chores and challenges (and occasionally as crises), all of which demand resolution.

The entire process of problem solving is fundamental to being human. So is the process of *sharing* the experience. When we communicate the experience of solving the problem, we do it linearly—we recreate the problem for the next person in line and that person gets to experience it too, albeit vicariously.

Essentially, the storyteller only needs to answer three questions: What's happening? Who is it happening to? And why should we care? What's happening is plot (problem). Who it's happening to is character (person). And why we should care is the emotional heart of the story—the most important part.

After that, the storyteller needs only one skill: *effective communication.*

Effective communication is not about giving the reader a totally detailed and completely accurate description of events. Effective communication is not about eloquent language and elegant metaphor. Effective communication is simply about *evoking the experience.*

First, you create the experience for yourself—then you share what it feels like. The reader recreates it. All you need to provide the reader are the elements *essential to the emotional moment.*

This is why rage was such a good fuel for me to start with. Everybody knows rage. And everybody can plug into rage very easily. If you write from rage, the reader will access his own in response. This is why some of the most effective stories ever written have a strong component of anger in them—it's a familiar, easy, and powerful emotional hook.

But while rage is an effective place to write from, it isn't the *best* place to write from, because if rage is the highest emotion a writer can aspire to, then there are whole dimensions of emotional power *beyond* rage that he or she is missing. The challenge is always to look beyond the limits.

So when I finished being angry with my "first-best writing instructor" (sometime in 1969 or 1981 or 1992, somewhere around there, I think), I had to find another fuel. It took a while—several years, in fact—but I found something better than simple rage, something so much more powerful that a single dose of it has been good for twenty years *and I'm still accelerating.* Since I discovered the source of this better fuel, I've written twenty more TV scripts and twenty more books—some of the best work in my life.

So what is this superfuel?

It's the next step beyond *enthusiasm.*

Of all the things I've ever learned about writing, this is the most important: There's a domain of excitement and eagerness and delight that can be astonishing. It is a place of commitment and discovery and wonderment. It is the far side of passion. It is a totality of purpose, an inspired obsession. I like to call it *stardrive*. It's the engine at the center of your personal starship. It's your *heart of brightness*. It is who you really are. It is simply you—*you are the source*.

If you've already been there, then you know what I mean. And if you haven't been there yet, or if you're not sure . . . don't panic. Start writing anyway. Write what you care about most—that way at least one person in the universe loves your story. (And if one person loves it, then surely there will be others.)

If you can do that, then somewhere along the way, *I promise*, you will ignite the engines of your enthusiasm in ways that will astonish you. You have a natural ability to communicate. Every human being does. What we call creativity is no more than your willingness to fully express yourself as passionately and as honestly as you can.

Write from your heart and you will go into stardrive.

May the source be with you.
—David Gerrold

The Literature of Imagination

The distinguishing characteristic of fantastic literature is that it evokes a sense of wonder in the audience.

Start with a simple exercise.

Actually take the time to do this—not as a thought experiment, but as a specific physical writing process. It'll be more effective that way.

Take out a blank piece of paper (or open a new file on your computer), and make a list of your favorite science fiction and fantasy movies.

List all the ones that changed the way you thought about things, that made you want to know more—the ones where you left the theater reluctantly because what you really wanted to do was climb into the screen and go back into the world of the movie.

Here's my list:

The Wizard of Oz
King Kong (1933)
The 5000 Fingers of Dr. T
Them!
War of the Worlds
20,000 Leagues Under the Sea
Forbidden Planet
Invasion of the Body Snatchers (1956)

A Midsummer Night's Dream (Jiri Trnka animated version)
Slaughterhouse-Five
Kwaidan
Yellow Submarine
Planet of the Apes
2001: A Space Odyssey
The Exorcist
Star Wars
Aliens
The Adventures of Buckaroo Banzai Across the Eighth Dimension
Repo Man
The Princess Bride

Now make a list of your favorite science fiction and fantasy books.

List all the ones that seemed to be written especially for you; the stories that took you to marvelous new worlds—stories that awoke new feelings in you, and took you to places you never wanted to leave.

Here's my list:

1984 by George Orwell
Brave New World by Aldous Huxley
What Mad Universe by Frederic Brown
The Stars My Destination by Alfred Bester
Starship Troopers by Robert A. Heinlein
The Moon Is A Harsh Mistress by Robert A. Heinlein
Dune by Frank Herbert
Dragonflight by Anne McCaffrey
Ringworld by Larry Niven
The Hobbit by J.R.R. Tolkien
The Left Hand of Darkness by Ursula K. LeGuin
The Dying Earth by Jack Vance

Watership Down by Richard Adams
Inferno by Larry Niven and Jerry Pournelle
A Wizard of Earthsea by Ursula K. LeGuin
Bridge of Birds by Barry Hughart
The Door Into Fire by Diane Duane
The Long Run by Daniel Keys Moran
Discworld (the entire series) by Terry Pratchett
Hyperion by Dan Simmons

Now look at your lists.

Do you remember how you felt the first time you saw these fantastic films? Do you remember what you felt as you turned the pages of a story you were falling in love with?

Do you remember those feelings? The flavors? The emotions you felt? Can you recreate them now, sitting in your chair? Close your eyes for a moment and see which of those images are still floating in your mind. What sensations do they still evoke in you today?

Probably, the first time you saw the movies on your list, or read the books, you were struck with feelings of awe and astonishment. Probably, you were surprised and amazed. Perhaps you even gasped or cried out in startled reaction.

Perhaps these were things you had never seen before, never even imagined. Perhaps your imagination was stretched beyond its limits, stretched and *expanded*. And afterward, perhaps you were left pondering things far beyond your sense of the possible.

That feeling is the *sense of wonder*.

The literature of the fantastic is about awakening that feeling of awe—*and exercising it.*

The *sense of wonder* is the marvelous heart of every great science fiction or fantasy story. It comes from the *surprise* of discovery. It comes from the recognition of the magic within. Most of all, it comes from the realization—the *acknowledgment*—of something new in the universe.

That sense of wonder is what you aspire to create; that's what you *must* create if you are going to write effective science fiction and fantasy.

Inventing Wonder

*Effective storytelling is about surprising
the audience. The rest is details.*

Your goal, as a storyteller, is to *evoke* the sense of wonder
in your audience.

You start by evoking the sense of wonder in yourself.
Where one person is awestruck, others are also likely to
be amazed.

Think of it this way: Your own head is your test lab, so
you have to wake up your own imagination first, drag it
out of bed, force it outside, barefoot, shivering in its paja-
mas, to look up at the dark blazing sky. There is no better
way to apply CPR to a snoozing imagination than by con-
fronting it with a skyful of dazzling stars and a bright gib-
bous moon.

Yes, you think you know what the sky looks like—but
go outside and look at it again. It will surprise you. Every
time.

And in that moment of surprise, that's when you are
most alive. Your astonished intake of breath is you listening
to the universe. Evoke that awe when you share the
moment.

Your job is to look for *surprises* in the world. And share
them.

To surprise someone, you have to bring new things to
his attention, or new ways of looking at old things. You
have to do the opposite of what's expected. You have to
startle. You can startle either with the shock of the alien

or the shock of recognition—or both at the same time. Startlement comes when something is unexpected.

Think about the fantastic movies and books you listed. They all have one thing in common: They're full of surprises—all sizes, all shapes, all flavors. That's what hooks the interest of the audience—all those marvelous new discoveries and possibilities.

Readers look for the surprises in your story the same way a child looks for the prize inside a box of Cracker Jacks. If you don't surprise your audience, they walk away from your story wondering why they bothered.

A great story is a series of surprises. Every chapter should have a surprise, every paragraph should have a surprise, every *sentence* should have a surprise.

If–The Most Powerful Word

It doesn't take a powerful lever to pry open the doors of imagination, just a well-applied one.

Before we can understand the *differences* between writing science fiction and writing fantasy (or the similarities), we have to examine what's unique to each of the forms. Science fiction first:

A science fiction story is an extrapolation of what we know about how the universe works. The classic definition of science fiction is that a story is based on one of two possible extrapolations: "What if . . . ?" or "If this goes on. . . ."

Notice that both starting places include the word *if*. In fact, *every* science fiction story starts with an *if*:

- *If* beings from another world decided to invade Earth, how would they do it?
- *If* a computer could achieve sentience, what would it think about?
- *What if* we could hang a cable from orbit down to the surface of Earth and run elevators up and down it?
- *If* someone fell asleep for a hundred years, what would the world be like when he woke up?
- *If* John F. Kennedy had gone into acting instead of politics, and if he had ended up playing the captain on *Star Trek*, what would the sixties have been like?

- *If* you had a belt that let you travel backward and forward in time, what would you do? Where would you go?
- *What if* human beings had three sexes? What would families be like?
- *If* faster-than-light travel was possible, what would war in space look like?
- *If* telepathy was real, how would telepaths live in our society?
- *If* an asteroid were on a collision course with Earth, how would humanity react?
- *If* a science fiction writer suspected that his adopted child might be a Martian, what would he do to find out for sure?
- *If* vampires were real, what would the scientific basis be for their condition?
- *If* some people started mutating into a different form of humanity, how would the rest of us react?
- *If* we could put a colony on the moon, what would we have to do to make it self-sustaining?

Notice how each of these story ideas begins with the assumption of possibility. The next step is to extrapolate the circumstances from the possibility. That's the science part in science fiction; sometimes it's one of the so-called "hard" sciences like physics, mathematics, astronomy, or biology; sometimes it's one of the "soft" sciences like history or sociology or linguistics. Many times it's a complex mixture of many sciences, all in one story.

But remember: *The most important part of science fiction is the science*. Otherwise it isn't *science* fiction.

Science

*A true scientist doesn't believe anything.
He is the ultimate agnostic. He is all
question and no answer.*

Unfortunately, a lot of people seem to think science is just another kind of *magic*. Or worse, they think that science is a kind of religion, and that it's just a different kind of *faith*. Or that science is *mutable*, and that reality can be voted on. Some people even think that science is the enemy of religion. No, it is not any of those things.

Science is an access to knowledge. It is a rigorous and unforgiving discipline. It is unsentimental—it discards old ideas on the trash heap of history as fast as they are discredited.[1] It accepts new concepts only so far as they explain the facts at hand better than the old ones.

Science is *not*—as some people think—the place where answers are found. It is the place where *questions* are asked. Science is not about knowledge—it is about ignorance, because science is about nothing if it is not about the *search* for greater knowledge. In science, an answer is only the place where you stopped asking the question.[2]

The core of science is the scientific method—a procedure for determining the difference between knowledge and belief.

[1] "The great tragedy of Science—the slaying of a beautiful hypothesis by an ugly fact."—Aldous Huxley
[2] "Truth in science can be defined as the working hypothesis best suited to open the way to the next better one."—Konrad Lorens

Belief is kind of like wishing. It exists inside yourself. It's a derivation of what psychologists call "magical thinking." Belief is a conviction that the universe works a certain way, even though you have no physical evidence at all to prove it, only your faith. Faith is useful, very useful, but it's not science.

Knowledge, on the other hand, is evidence. It exists outside yourself. It is measurable, it is testable, it is repeatable, and it is *demonstrable*. Most important, it can be communicated to other people. They can repeat the measurements and tests and demonstrate the same facts for themselves. In other words, knowledge is what we can all agree on, because we can each verify it for ourselves.

So the scientific method is *a procedure for determining the evidence*. It is a way of establishing agreement.

It works like this: You observe a phenomenon of some kind—a condition, a behavior, a curiosity—something that you do not understand. Other people observe it too, so you know it exists, but you have no explanation for it. So you postulate a *theory*.

Is your theory accurate or not? How do you find out? You *test* it.

You design an experiment that allows you to test only that single question, nothing else; i.e., the only variable is the one you are testing; everything else is a constant from one test to the next.

Whatever the specific result of the experiment, it is always a success—because it always gives you information. It is either information about what works, or it is information about what doesn't work; but either way, the result of the experiment is a fact, and each fact is a piece of knowledge.

Even if the experiment confirms your theory, you're still not done. That's the annoying thing about science—you're *never* done. One of two things can happen: Either a better theory comes along and you throw out the old one, or another fact comes along that doesn't fit your theory and you have to come up with a new one.

So the scientific method is about asking the question, and asking it again, and asking it yet again. It's about testing the facts as well as the theory, *forever*. To the scientific mind, there is no end. Theories aren't proven, they are simply used—and only as long as they are useful.

A theory is a map of a specific terrain of knowledge. It's not the territory, it's just a representation of it. Depending on what we need to do, we specify what kind of a map we need. Road maps are different from weather maps, rainfall maps are different from geological survey maps, terrain maps are different from maps to movie stars' homes. Every map is useful for the purpose it was designed for—and useless for the purposes it was not designed for.

As the researchers in our world continue to refine the different maps of the terrain we've discovered, the various maps become more accurate and more useful, and we become more powerful in what we can accomplish. That's why we make maps, and that's what science is about—mapmaking.

Science Fiction . . .

*There are two parts to a science fiction story.
One is science. The other is fiction. The
excitement is in the mix.*

Most science fiction stories are about intelligent folks dealing with an unknown phenomenon. During the course of the story, the reader (if not the hero) discovers the nature of that phenomenon, whatever it is. In that regard, a science fiction story is a lot like a murder mystery. We follow the detective as he figures out who the killer is—only in science fiction, the mystery involves much more than a dead body on the living room floor. The mystery is some facet of the universe that we haven't yet included in our maps.

Here's the good news. You don't have to be a scientist to write effective science fiction, but you do need to be enthused about the adventure of discovery. In science fiction, the sense of wonder comes as an internal *klunk* of recognition.

The bad news. It's not enough to be wonderful, it also has to be believable.

Here's an example. The planet Tatooine, as portrayed in *Star Wars*, is shown as a vast desert, with nothing growing anywhere. It's desolate and dry and uninhabitable. But if nothing grows there, where does the oxygen come from? How do the inhabitants breathe?

And if nothing grows there, how do banthas survive? Those things are as big as elephants. You find elephants on the savanna, on grasslands, in forests, and jungles—where there is plenty of greenery for them to graze. You don't find elephants in deserts. *A bantha is an elephant in a hair shirt. What does it eat?*

(Please don't send me letters explaining how it all works. I can do that exercise myself if I need to. But if you can figure out how to feed a bantha on a desert planet, then you've already learned one of the most important lessons of writing effective science fiction: world-building.)

The first issue in any science fiction story is believability. Because science fiction is rooted in science—*what we actually know about the way the universe works*—the writer has a responsibility to stay consistent with that body of knowledge. Assume the reader is at least as smart as you are. Assume that your audience has just as much experience with the real world. Don't contradict what is already known. You cannot rewrite the laws of physics and expect the reader to believe that your story is possible. (Sometimes you can cheat a little, like Wile E. Coyote, but that's a different discussion.)

Readers come to your story wanting to believe. To create believability, you have to believe in it yourself—because if you don't believe in it, how can anyone else?

If you write about a creature as big as a tank, like a bantha, then let us know what it eats—and what wants to eat it. How does it mate? How do the offspring survive? And if you really want to convince us that you know this creature well, show us the size of its droppings. (Remember the scene with the triceratops in *Jurassic Park*?)

This doesn't mean that you have to explain everything in your story down to the last niggling little detail. Otherwise your hero has to be Murray the Explainer. But whenever you postulate something in your science fiction world, take a moment to ask a few necessary questions about it.

Theodore Sturgeon used to encourage would-be writers

(and everyone else as well) to *ask the next question*. It was one of his best sermons and one of the best lessons a story-teller could learn. He used to wear a medallion of a Q with an arrow through it—his symbol for "Ask the next question." He gave that speech almost everywhere he went, and especially anytime anyone asked what the medallion meant.

He used to say, "The writer has to know what is in every nook and cranny of the story. You don't have to write it all down, but if you know what's there, it'll show."

So *after you build it, you have to move into it*. You have to look around, listen, taste, touch, smell, and *feel* what you have created—then report back, so the reader can feel it too. The reader wants to see the scenery, hear the music, taste the spices, pet the critters, smell the air, and most of all, he wants to feel the emotions. This is the *excitement of* science fiction: It gives the reader a chance to be someone else for a while—someone profoundly different; someone in a different universe, facing different challenges.

This is why science fiction and fantasy are sometimes called *escape literature*. They provide escape from reality—but in the hands of a good storyteller, the literature of imagination is also an access to something much more profound. Consider this thought:

Who you think you are is determined by the time and place in which you live.

Context is the largest part of identity—you know who you are by measuring yourself against your surroundings. A person living in a different world is going to have a different sense of who she is and what relationships are possible to her. The stranger the world, the stranger the forces working on the person, and the more bizarre the shape that person's identity will be bent into. And so, too the author of that world:

As you create your story, it takes on a reality of its own—and as you explore its workings, *you* metamorphose. Your thinking changes, your perceptions shift, you become a different person: You become the kind of person who can tell *this* story from the inside. If you succeed, then the way you describe events and places and characters will be as a resident would describe it, and it will feel to the reader as if you've been there yourself.

. . . and Fantasy

Science fiction is about what's possible.
Fantasy is about what's not. Fantasy is harder.

Where science fiction has a foundation rooted in the scientific knowledge of the real world, fantasy seems to have no such grounding at all. Fantasy looks like the abandonment of the laws of science. The map says, "Here there be dragons." Meaning: All previous statutes are null and void. They no longer apply. They've been repealed.

That's what it *looks like.*

Dig deeper.

Like science fiction, fantasy also starts out with an *if:*

- *What if* you found a book in the library that taught you how to be a wizard?
- *If* rabbits had a culture, what kind of legends would they have?
- *What if* a hobbit had to throw a magic ring into a volcano to save the world from evil?
- *If* a vampire gave an interview, what kind of story would he tell?
- *What if* a man's best friend was a six-foot-tall invisible rabbit?
- *If* the world was on the back of a giant turtle swimming through space, would NASA be launching spaceships to determine the sex of the turtle?
- *If* a little girl fell into a mirror, what would she find on the other side?
- *What if* the animals had a revolution and kicked all

the humans off the farm and ran it themselves?
- *What if* a ghost was still in love with his wife?
- *What if* talking cats had to save New York City from a dimension-hopping evil spirit in the shape of a T. Rex?
- *What if* people started turning into rhinoceroses?
- *What if* people started turning green?
- *What if* people started growing fur all over their bodies?
- *What if* people suddenly started being born with tails?
- *What if* a man woke up one morning and found he had turned into a giant cockroach?
- *What if* a husband and wife could trade bodies, so each could see what the other's life was like?
- *If* human beings could wrap themselves into cocoons like caterpillars, what would they metamorphose into?
- *What if* a little boy fell into Santa's bag of toys?
- *What if* your teddy bear came to life?
- *What if* a talking dog, a telepathic duck, and a psychokinetic rabbit had the winning lotto ticket, but a malicious wizard was determined to turn them all into animal crackers?

Do you notice the difference here between science fiction and fantasy?

There is no limit to what you can postulate in fantasy. You can get pretty silly if you want. Or you can get poignant, or satirical, or go for sheer epic grandeur. You can do allegory, metaphor, myth, or just sheer absurdity and leave it for the reader to figure out if it means anything.

When you ask a science fiction question, the first thing you have to do is root it in reality; you have to explain to yourself *why* it's possible, so you can believe in it yourself.

In a fantasy story, you assume it's already possible, and you don't bother explaining the how or the why. In that respect, fantasy seems to offer much more freedom to the author: *freedom from explaining*. Go ahead, make something up! Anything. After all, this is fantasy, right?

Wrong.

The audience *still* wants to believe in your world—and believability comes from the recognition of an internally consistent system of logic. If things are not consistent, they are (literally!) *unbelievable*.

This is not some arbitrary rule. It's how the human mind works. The mind looks for connections. The mind synthesizes patterns as a key to comprehension. *The mind insists on structure*. Lack of structure is chaos. Without it, the mind flails. And if there is no immediately discernable structure, *the mind makes stuff up*—whatever is convenient, to fill the gap.

Don't take my word for it. *Test it yourself*.

Go out and ask people questions that you know they couldn't possibly know the answer to. "Who really killed Kennedy?" "Why was the third season of the original *Star Trek* so awful?" "When will he write the fifth book?" Out of a hundred people, you will be lucky to find five who are honest enough to say, "I don't know." The rest will make something up. Most people would rather die than admit they don't know something.

Try it. If you ever needed evidence of the mind's desperate need to create structure, it's always right there in front of you. Ask any human being a question that you know he or she can't answer. The human mind cannot stand not knowing something—it would rather have a wrong answer than no answer at all. So it'll grab the first idea it can, no matter how preposterous it might be . . . like a drowning man grabbing for the first anvil he sees.

The result is not information. It is misinformation. It is noise. It does not bring you closer to understanding—it pushes you farther away, because now there is all the made-up stuff you have to disregard before you can find out what's so.

What does this have to do with storytelling?

Simply this: If you don't have answers to the questions that your story engenders, you are casting your readers adrift in a sea of chaos. The reader will not understand what your story is really about or what it is you are trying to accomplish. Your job is to be the vessel, the sails, the compass, and the wind. Your job is to be the sight of land on the horizon. Because—

Fantasy is not the abandonment of logic. It is the reinvention of it. A believable fantasy is the creation of an *alternate* structure of logic. Fantasy is not simply the stuff you make up. Fantasy requires an underlying structure to unify your ideas. Like science, fantasy represents a consistent pattern of knowledge; the difference is that the fantasy map is not designed to map accurately to the real world.

Almost all fantasy relies on *personification*—that is, whatever happens in a fantasy, there is an anthropomorphic reason, *a causative agency:*

> "Who turns out the light in the refrigerator?"
> "A little man who lives inside, called Yehudi."

> "Dammit, why won't this car start?"
> "Gremlins."

> "Say a prayer to the god of parking places, otherwise we'll have to walk from the far end of the lot."

> "Why is Lennie so stupid?"
> "The brain fairy left a quarter under his pillow."

"Make the stoplight change."
"I can't. It doesn't like you."

"You have to sacrifice a book to the television set, otherwise it'll only show reruns."

Nothing ever happens by accident in the fantasy world. Some phenomenon—supernatural or magic or otherwise—is responsible. *This is the logic of fantasy.* Fantasy is about the assignment of consciousness and reason. In fantasy, everything is conscious, or at least potentially conscious—animals, plants, rocks, machines, the wind. *Everything.*

The logic of fantasy grows out of the surreal logic of the human mind. The human mind is not by nature scientific. Rational thinking is a learned skill. (The front page of your daily newspaper should be regarded as evidence of this. Most minds are still untrained.)

Mind-logic starts as soon as children start learning to talk. As soon as they start associating symbols with things, they start trying to manipulate things by the symbols that connect to them. You teach a child a word, he believes the word has power over the thing. This is called "magical thinking." *If I wish real hard for something, it'll happen. I mustn't wish anything awful or it will happen. Step on a crack and you'll break your mother's back.*

"Magical thinking" presumes that the symbol that represents an object controls it, so what happens to the symbol, happens to the object (e.g., stick a pin in a voodoo doll and your worst enemy gets stabbing pains). This is the kind of logic that the immature mind uses as it tries to grasp some control over the physical universe. It doesn't work, but it takes most people about eight or nine years to figure that out. Some never do.

And because the mind has a great deal of difficulty pre-
suming that anything ever happens without a mind as a
causative agent, everything in the universe is therefore
either alive or under the control of something alive. *There's
a monster living in the closet. There are monsters under
my bed. If I pull the covers over my head, they won't find
me.* The mind, in becoming aware of itself, presumes that
everything else *is also mind.*

As the individual grows, the mind develops other, more
sophisticated logics. Some are bizarre, twisted, ugly, dangerous, and psychotic. Others are charming, eccentric,
addled, fascinating, mysterious, oblique, and esoteric.
There are many different systems of logic, and we step into
the ones that serve us best—or that we *think* serve us best.

Most religions are built on self-contained systems of
logic. Many human-resource courses present ways to train
the mind in the logic of effectiveness. There are whole systems of psychology built around different definitions of
mind-logic. But it's *all* mind-logic. *Everything.* (Including
this book.) The mind is always trying to figure out how to
work the universe, and it's always inventing logical constructions to apply.

It is this need for logic that is the source of all fantasy:
"If I go to the bathroom now, the phone will ring." "If I
get the car washed, it'll rain." "If I say the right prayers,
God will grant my wish." "If I take personal responsibility
for this, I can make it happen." The latter statement, at
least, has a kernel of power in it.

(To be bluntly pragmatic about the whole thing: To the
extent that any system empowers you to produce results,
it works; to the extent that it defeats you and keeps you
from producing results, it doesn't. If you believe it, it's true
for you. If you don't believe it, it's superstition.)

Every great fantasy is built on a perceivable system of

logic that—no matter how silly it might seem in the rational world—is still complete and consistent unto itself. If you have talking dogs in your story, then cats probably talk as well. If the wind whispers advice to your hero, then the brook probably babbles madly to itself. If vampires are afraid of crosses, then holy water probably burns them. If death for humans is a human-sized ghostly figure in a black hood carrying a scythe, then death for rats is a rat-sized figure in similar garb. If magic words can make supernatural things happen, then mispronouncing a magic word will have disastrous and dangerous results. If automobiles have souls, then airplanes do too. If the toaster can talk, then so can the vacuum cleaner. If there are no leprechaun nuns, then Paddy kissed a penguin. If Superman came from Krypton, then anyone else coming from Krypton will also have super powers. If Martian wishes can make stoplights change, then Martian wishes can also win a Hugo Award. If the washing machine has a sock-digester, then the dryer has a button-remover. Elevators travel in groups because only one of them knows the way. You'll find it in the last place you look. And never play cards with a man named Doc. If you're a police dog, show me your badge. Fantasy works by its own rules—*but it does have rules.*

You can make up any rules you want for your fantasy story— but once you set those rules, *you are bound by them.* You cannot break them; you cannot change them midway through the book. Doing that betrays the trust of the audience. Remember: If you are creating a world, you are behaving like a god—and gods don't cheat.

Both science fiction and fantasy take you to worlds that don't exist. Both require strict adherence to the rules and structures of believability. The difference is that science fiction is rooted in the logic of the physical universe, and fantasy is rooted in the logic of the personal universe—the logic of the mind. It is the reader's perception of a structure of underlying logic that makes a story credible.

The reader will suspend disbelief—he won't suspend common sense.[3]

---

[3] If E.T. could fly at the end of the movie to get away, why didn't he fly away at the beginning?

What Is a Story?

*If you don't know what a story is,
how can you write one?*

Here's an exercise:
Don't peek ahead.

Take a blank piece of paper, or open a new file on your computer.

Type this:

A story is

Now finish the sentence. Write down your definition of a story. In as few words as possible, say *exactly* what you think a story is.

Be as clear and concise as you can.

Don't worry about trying to get the *right* answer. There is no *right* answer. There is no *wrong* answer. There is only what you think. So just write down what you think a story should accomplish.

Pretend you have to explain it to someone else. What do you have to say to have another person understand what storytellers do?

Don't peek ahead.

Write it down.

Rewrite as necessary.

Do it now.

WHAT IS A STORY?

Here's one answer:

A story is about a journey.

Here's another answer:

A story is about a healing.

And one more:

A story is about a transformation.

None of these are the right answer. None of these are the wrong answer. None of these are the *official* answer, because none of these are the *only* answer.

The point of the exercise is to have you determine for yourself what result you are trying to achieve. You have to know your goal—otherwise you'll never recognize it when you achieve it. And you'll never know why if you keep missing it.

A Story Is . . .

Plato said, "The unexamined life is not worth living." The obvious corollary is, "The unlived life is not worth examining."

A story is about a problem.

A story is about a person with a problem—but first, it's about *the problem*.

The person in the story, the character, is the demonstration of the problem. The protagonist is the *expression* of the problem.

In a story, this person has this problem because he or she was designed for it. But as a writer, you work for believability, so you want to design your character's relationship with the problem to look like the kind of relationships people have with problems in real life.

In real life, people have problems because they *choose* them.

Huh?

How do you choose a problem?

It's easy. *Abdicate your responsibility.*

When you give up responsibility in the matter, you create it as a problem. Resist handling the situation, and it persists.

Werner Erhard, creator of the now-retired *est* training, one of the first personal-effectiveness courses (a particularly interesting paradigm that demonstrated that the mind works like a machine), defined a problem as "a situation you are putting up with or trying to change." A problem is something you're uncomfortable with. His answer was a very eloquent version of, "Get over it."

Most problems are created when someone says, "I can't handle it." Or: "I don't want to get involved." "I don't want to have this conversation." "I'm sorry sir, that's not my table." *A problem is created every time you avoid taking responsibility for your part.* The situation *doesn't* get resolved; resolution gets postponed and the situation gets *worse*. It endures until the person dies . . . or gets uncomfortable enough and annoyed enough to do something.

Usually, the handling of the problem is much less trouble than all the agitation and anxiety that leads up to it. The real problem is not the situation itself—*it is the mind's resistance to handling it.*

That's how *you* choose a problem, that's how your protagonist *chooses* a problem: By resisting the situation. By looking at circumstances and saying, *"I can't handle it."*

So in life, as well as in fiction, a person's problems are the direct result of how he or she chooses to behave. What you choose to handle, you handle. What you choose to not handle becomes the problem you get to live with day after day after day. And the longer you refuse to handle a situation, the worse it gets.

What you resist, persists.

The story is about the details.

First, it's about the details of resistance; then it's about the details of acceptance, discovery, and interaction; and finally, it's about the details of resolution. So storytelling is about creating interesting problems—looking to see *why* they are problems, looking to see why the hero has made this a problem, looking to see what the hero has to give up, and finally what the hero has to become to resolve the problem.

The bad news is that the writer has to become the kind

of person who can solve problems. *The writer* has to learn how to say, *"I can handle this."*

Have you ever noticed, in the movies, when the hero finally makes up his mind to handle the situation, the problem (and the movie) is over in ten minutes? Real life works a lot like that too. At least for most problems it does.

But sometimes handling the situation *isn't* that easy. Sometimes it's complex. Sometimes it looks to be beyond your ability. Sometimes it looks impossible. That's what makes the situation *interesting*—the complications. Especially if there are surprises inside.

The bigger the problem, the bigger the character has to be to solve it.

In fact, for your story to be important enough to justify telling, it should be about the biggest problem your character has ever faced. And if it isn't the biggest problem, then why are you telling *this* story? Why aren't you telling *that* story?

The one significant exception to this rule is an episodic television series. In a series, the problem in each episode is almost always someone else's. The protagonist of the show is only there to be a catalyst for the resolution *of someone else's problem*. He is an outsider, an observer. His participation in the moral dilemma is as a facilitator. (The Yiddish word for this is *kibitzer*.) He is a meddler. And the job of the television scriptwriter is to justify the hero's meddling.

Rarely can an episodic television series allow its star characters to be the person with the problem—because if this situation is the biggest and most significant problem in his life, *then what do you do in the next episode?*

Afterwards, everything else is anticlimactic. It's of such less significance that there's no reason to tell it, is there?

So choose your problem carefully. Choose the biggest one you can create. Your hero is going to be stuck with it.

Crises and Challenges

Failure is when you don't get up again.

There are two kinds of problems that human beings face in life—*crises* and *challenges*.

A *crisis* is a situation that you didn't choose, but it demands to be handled *now!* Most crises start out as chores, simple little problems that persist primarily because you don't want to handle them. The more you resist handling a chore, the worse it gets. Eventually, it becomes a *crisis*—and then you don't have a choice in the matter anymore. You're trapped in the situation.

A *challenge* is a problem that you create for yourself because you are excited by the possibility. Writing a story is a challenge. Building a bridge is a challenge. Raising a child is a challenge. (And sometimes a chore and a crisis.) Challenges are problems that you *consciously choose.*

Both kinds of problems are interesting and exciting— and both require that the person at the core of the story grow teeth big enough to chew the problem. Both require growth on the part of the hero.

But each kind of problem creates a different kind of story. A story about a crisis that must be handled *now* sets a deadline on the hero. The clock is running. That automatically creates enormous tension for the audience. Can the astronauts blow up the asteroid before it hits the

Earth? Will Van Helsing find Dracula's coffin before sunset? Will Frodo toss the ring into the volcano before Sauron's power is too strong to resist? Will Jim McCarthy find out the secret of the Chtorrans before the Earth's resources are overcome? Tick tock, tick tock, tick tock. . . .

A crisis demands action. The character is under fire, and he has to demonstrate the inner core of his strength, his wit, and his cleverness. *Or die.* Usually, the resolution is a frightening demonstration of his anger at the circumstance. Often he takes revenge upon his enemies.

A challenge, however, is a task that a character has freely chosen. He doesn't have to take on the challenge but he does so anyway—and because it's a conscious choice, made without duress, the relationship with the task is a much more personal expression of who the hero is and what he is committed to. It is the demonstration of a higher level of passion.

In a "challenge" story, the hero is usually trying to build something or discover something. In Arthur C. Clarke's *The Fountains of Paradise*, the hero is building an orbital elevator. In Sir Arthur Conan Doyle's *The Lost World*, Professor Challenger is searching for dinosaurs in the Amazon. In Jules Verne's *From the Earth to the Moon*, the heroes are attempting the first manned space flight. In Heinlein's *The Rolling Stones*, the Stone family has bought a spaceship to become space traders and ferry supplies to Mars.

Some of the very best stories combine elements of both crisis and challenge. The protagonist takes on a challenge only to have it grow out of control and become a crisis. *Apollo 13*, for instance, is such a story. So is *Frankenstein*. And even *The Lord of the Rings*. These kinds of situations challenge and confront the protagonist from all sides, and they provide enormous excitement for the reader.

Once your character embarks, he or she is likely to encounter both kinds of situations. From the storyteller's perspective, every circumstance must be approached as an opportunity to make discoveries about the nature of the world—*and the hero*.

A character who gets to deal with both kinds of situations is much more interesting to the reader. How a character deals with crises and challenges reveals who he or she really is.

Or to put it bluntly: *What you do is who you are*. What you say you're up to is who you think you are. But what you *do* is who you *really* are.

Ask your character these two questions: Who are you? Who do you want to be?

Ask them of yourself as well.

The Hero

Whoever your attention stays focused on, that's who the story is about. That's the agreement you have with the audience.

One of the most insightful critics of science fiction and fantasy was a fellow named James Blish. He wrote some of the best fantasy and science fiction novels of the forties and fifties, including *Cities in Flight, Surface Tension, Black Easter,* and the Hugo-winning classic, *A Case of Conscience.* The essential quality of all of his work was that his heroes weren't just solving a physical problem; they were almost always caught on the crux of a moral or ethical dilemma created by their role in the situation. During much of the sixties and seventies, Blish served as the book reviewer for *The Magazine of Fantasy and Science Fiction.* He demanded that writers live up to the challenges they set for themselves, and he was a major voice holding the genre's feet to the fire. (And when James Blish held your feet to the fire, you deserved it. Here, I'll show you the scars. . . .)

Blish was also a very kind man, very much committed to the success of young writers. One evening, he gave me a piece of advice so profound that it transformed my own writing.

"Who does it hurt?" he asked. *"That's who your story is about."*

Right there, in those two sentences, he encapsulated enough writing wisdom on which to build a whole career.

If you never learn anything else about heroism, it doesn't matter—that's the important lesson. *Who does it hurt? And why?*

The beginning of your story is about the *who*. You have to show the audience everything they need to know about who this person is.

The middle is about the *why*. You have to show the audience everything they need to know about how this problem works and why it belongs to *this* person.

The end is about the *what*. What does this person do to resolve the hurt? And if you've taken care of the *who* and the *why*, then the *what* will be obvious. (The trick is making it surprising as well.)

Most writers start out with an idea first:

> *What if* Earth was invaded by giant, pink, man-eating caterpillars?

Who does it hurt? Everybody. Who does it hurt *the most?* Whose hurt is *most* interesting? *Who* is going to be present to the most important parts of the story?

Let's say there's a young woman in Oregon whose horse gets eaten by the first giant caterpillar. Is she the most important person? Is she going to be present to the rest of the invasion? Or is she just scenery for the rest of the tale?

Maybe there's a man in Show Low, Arizona, who takes the first video pictures of the aliens when four giant worms attack his town. Is he the hero? Or are his pictures useful details for someone else?

Perhaps there's a scientist in Denver who is assigned to capture one of the aliens. Will she be available to the most critical parts of the story?

Oh, wait—here's an idea. Let's start where *War of the Worlds* leaves off. If Earth bacteria are fatal to Martians, then alien bacteria should be fatal to humans. So maybe, before we start seeing the giant pink caterpillars, there are plagues that wipe out half the human race. That means that the various military services will not be immediately able to respond, and the problem of dealing with the invasion will fall to the survivors of the plagues; they'll have to train themselves as they learn from their mistakes. But who's the best person to follow? An army captain who builds a guerrilla force? A civilian who learns how to survive by cooperating with the aliens? An advisor to the president? Could the story be about someone who has the opportunity to experience *all* of those situations? Who would that person be?

It should be the one who *hurts* the most.

My answer to the question is that the hero is someone in his late teens, halfway through college, living with expectations of a normal life—suddenly, civilization breaks down around him, most of his family dies, and he gets drafted into a desperate army. He's emotionally tangled, lost, frustrated, angry, and grieving. And he doesn't understand how fast the world is changing around him—at least not until he gets hit over the head with the unpleasant truth. And because he studied some science in college, his duties are not just to kill the aliens, but to help capture them alive and bring them to Denver for study. The creatures fascinate him; he ends up with divided loyalties—one foot in the war and one foot in alien research. This is the basis for my alien invasion series, *The War Against the Chtorr*.

Early on in the planning, I realized that this story had many elements of epic scale. So the important thing was to create a hero who would experience the whole vast panorama of events. I wanted a hero who could go out in the field and see how the alien ecology is spreading across the planet. He would have to come back and report to both military and scientific agencies and see how the various branches were responding. He would have to meet with the president's own task force to see what the nation's leaders were thinking. Ultimately, perhaps he would even be captured by renegade humans or by the aliens themselves and live among them for a while, so he could gain insights that weren't available any other way.[4]

The hero doesn't have to be the most important person on the planet—just a person who gets shoved into enough situations that he will experience the scale of the problem. He should meet many people, all of who are reacting to the situation in different ways, each one *dramatizing* a different facet of the human condition.

Let's talk about that word *drama.*

Drama is conflict. Conflict is drama. The two words mean the same thing: *confrontation.*

Conflict is confrontation—two things in opposition.

The more different situations the hero stumbles into, the more people he meets, the greater are his opportunities for confrontation—and out of that, you get to demonstrate not only his problem but his *character* as well.

How does your hero deal with confrontation? Does this person react with anger, panic, outrage, sorrow, or amusement? Does this person resist or engage? Does this person enjoy the challenge or does he or she panic in the face of crisis?

You need to ask these questions in every situation. Asking these questions brings each scene to life:

Why is this moment important? *Where* is the pain? *Why* does it hurt? And most important—*what* will make it *worse?*

The job of the storyteller is to put the hero up a tree

---

[4] *The War Against The Chtorr: A Matter For Men, A Day For Damnation, A Rage For Revenge, A Season For Slaughter,* and someday *A Method For Madness.*

and then throw rocks at him. Surround the tree with rabid wolves. Light it on fire. Put a helicopter above with bad guys firing laser-sighted explosive rounds. Have an earthquake. The volcano blows up. Drop an asteroid on the planet. Aliens invade. And the tree has Dutch elm disease.

If you're doing fantasy, put the hero up a tree, surround it with werewolves and put dragons in the sky. And the family curse is turning him into a frog. Meanwhile the druid who lives in the tree is having her period. . . . Whatever it takes.

One of the most stunning examples of this kind of writing was chapter ten of *A Private Cosmos*, the third book in Phillip Jose Farmer's *World of Tiers* series. It's a fantasy place with various strange races all inhabiting an old-west environment. The hero, Kickaha, is a prisoner of six renegade warriors from a caravan of traders. His hands are tied and he has no weapon. The guards are taking him somewhere by horseback, they're riding across the plains. Suddenly, coming from their left is a vast buffalo stampede. Suddenly, coming from their right is an angry tribe of half-horse/half-humans who are determined to kill Kickaha. Kickaha's captors start galloping madly to outrun the buffalo and the half-horses. One of the half-horses (who has personally sworn vengeance) throws a lance and Kickaha's horse goes down. Kickaha runs *toward* the stampeding buffalo and manages to grab hold of one of the animals and catapult himself onto its neck. Now (hands still tied) he's riding a buffalo stampede, with angry half-horses chasing him. To escape the half-horses, he jumps from the back of one charging buffalo onto the back of the next, and then again and again. But the angry half-horse chasing him jumps up on top of the buffalo stampede and starts leaping from one animal to the next too. . . . And just ahead, there are bad guys in an aircraft firing death rays at everybody.

Now, in chapter eleven. . . . (And if I remember correctly, the stampede is charging toward a cliff.)

The idea is to throw as many different kinds of rocks as possible. The name of the game is *Hurt the Hero!*

Why?

Because if he doesn't hurt, why should we care?

> On his way home from saving the planet, Superman picked up a carton of Double Double Chocolate Fudge Swirl, Lois's favorite flavor.

Why should we care about the planet or what it took to save it, if it's no more important than a carton of ice cream? (Granted, we're talking *chocolate* ice cream, but even so. . . .) Try it this way instead:

> If he didn't stop the asteroid from slamming into the Earth, everyone on the planet would die—including his beloved Lois. . . .

When you hurt the hero, you reveal his emotional core. If the hero's wife is being held hostage by Klingon terrorists, if his mother is dying of Martian measles, if his precious daughter is trapped in a chrono-synclastic-infundibulum, if the dog has mutated into a ghastly green amorphous blob that eats everything in its path, if the experimental black hole at CyberCore Labs has revealed itself to be a sentient being, and if all this happens simultaneously, then whichever of these issues the hero tends to *first*, tells you what is most important to him.

That's why it has to hurt. Because that's how we find out *who* the hero is.

Who Is This Person?

You can tell your whole life story in thirty seconds. It's a question of editing.

Try this exercise: Sit down with a blank piece of paper, or sit down at your computer, and answer these questions about your character:

- What is the character's name?
- How old is the character?
- Who were the character's parents?
- Where was the character born? What were the circumstances of the birth? Did anything unusual happen? What is the character's relationship with his/her/its parents/creators?
- What was the character's childhood like? Are there any brothers or sisters? What is the relationship with siblings?
- Where did the character go to school? What kind of education did the character have? How much education? Of what quality? What does the character know? What does he *not* know?
- What kinds of relationships does the character have? What kinds of friends? Enemies? Why?
- Does the character have any bad habits? Drugs? Alcohol? Tobacco? Sexual appetites? What character flaws does this person have?

- Describe the physical appearance of the character. Skin color? Height? Weight? Physique? Tall or short? Fat or thin or muscular?
- Hair color? (Baldness?) Eye color?
- Does the character have any disabilities? Distinguishing marks? Tattoos? Disfigurements? Why? What were the causative circumstances?
- What kind of jewelry or ornamentation does the character wear? Rings, earrings, necklace, medallion, or piercing?
- What class of person is this? Wealthy or poor? Honest or rogue? Soldier or leader? Merchant or laborer? Teacher or student? Highborn or lowborn? Educated or ignorant? Rational or superstitious? Religious or skeptical?
- What kind of clothing does the character wear? Fancy or plain? Expensive or cheap? Elegant or simple? Describe the clothes. What kind of footgear? What kind of leggings or skirt? What kind of shirt or blouse? What kind of coat? What kind of headgear?
- What kind of weapons does this character carry? Why? What do these weapons accomplish? How much training has your character had in the use of these weapons?
- What powers or abilities does this character have? What, if anything, is *special* about this character? What is fantastic?
- What does your character believe? What does he know? What does he need to know?
- What is the problem? *Why* is it his or her problem? Why does this problem *hurt*?
- What is this character's weakness? Fatal flaw?
- What is this character afraid of?
- What makes this character angry?

- What makes this character sad?
- What makes this character happy?
- What does this character want?
- What does this character *need?*
- What does this character most need to learn? What does this character most need to say? To whom?
- What is the essential emotional *problem* that this character must face and resolve?
- What other questions do you want to add to this list? Answer them too.

Answer as many of the questions as you can. Some of the questions might not be applicable. If you're writing about a nonhuman character, like a robot or an alien, you'll have to adjust the questions accordingly. Feel free to add any specific questions of your own that you think appropriate. Use the questions to write the most detailed description of your character that you can.

Now, the *fun* part.

Sit down at your computer and write a conversation between you and your character. Imagine yourself in a room appropriate to the situation. You and the character are sitting opposite each other. Start by thanking the character for participating. Establish a friendly relationship. (Remember, you're God in the universe you created, so be compassionate and generous of spirit.)

Ask the character everything you want to know. Don't worry if you don't know the answers; when you ask the question, the character will know and will answer honestly. Yes, sometimes it happens that a character turns recalcitrant and answers, "I don't want to say." If that happens, just move on to the next question—or you can ask the character "Why?" and see what he or she says. Whatever happens, keep the conversation going.

Now give the character the same opportunity to ask you everything he or she wants to know. Answer honestly. (You can't lie to your character anyway.)

Continue the conversation until both you and the character have asked every question you need to ask. Continue the conversation until both you and the character have said everything you need to say.

When there is nothing left to ask and nothing left to say, conclude the conversation by thanking the character. Let the character thank you in return. (Or not, as the case sometimes happens.)

I have done this exercise for over twenty years with writing students. Sometimes I've done this as an eyes-closed visualization exercise; I've read the questions aloud and the students have let the visualizations occur in response. Sometimes I've assigned it as a writing exercise. In both forms, the exercise always works—sometimes with humorous effect, more often with dramatic impact. (When I did this exercise with Jim McCarthy, the hero of my series, *The War Against the Chtorr*, we didn't get any talking done at all. As soon as I introduced myself, he leapt across the table and came after me with a knife. I barely escaped with my life.)

However the conversation works out, you will end up with a significantly enhanced understanding of who your character really is. Whenever you get stuck in your story, going to this exercise will get you unstuck very fast.

Setting the Stage

Scenery should explain itself.

The lights go down, the curtain goes up. The first thing you see is the scenery.

Notice how every science fiction movie or television show starts with a shot of the location where the story is about to occur. Movies that take place in outer space always start with a shot of stars and a starship. Movies that take place on another world always start with a shot of the planet. This is to let you know where you are.

Novels and stories start the same way. You have to give the reader a sense of where he is and what's happening as quickly as possible. You don't want to start the story by confusing the reader.

Some science fiction writers start out with a whole chapter explaining the planet; they tell you how big it is, whether the gravity is lighter or heavier, how long are the years, what the atmosphere is made of, what kind of seasons, what is the temperature range, what lives there, and even what color the sky appears to be. Some writers spend long chapters giving you detailed histories of the civilization, or explaining how the alien society works. Some stories need that kind of stage-setting, and an effective writer (Jack Vance, for example) knows how to hold the reader's interest while leisurely setting the stage; but for most writers—especially beginners—it's best to get into the story quickly and hold much of that exposition until later, when it's needed.

Show. Don't tell. As a general rule of thumb, you want to set the scene quickly, get the story in motion, and then explain as you go. What you're likely to find is that the more you show, the less you have to explain.

It's always better to demonstrate. Here are two paragraphs:

> "Pay attention, boys," the professor said. "You must be careful on the moon. Luna has only one-sixth the mass of Earth, so lunar gravity is proportionally less. If you're not used to it, you could hurt yourself."

> Stinky unfastened his safety harness and jumped out of his seat; almost immediately he bounced up and banged his head on the cabin ceiling. "Owwww!" he wailed as he dropped slowly back down.

Which one is more interesting? Which one gives you a better sense of lunar gravity? The first paragraph is a lecture; the second paragraph is storytelling. The first paragraph tells, but the second paragraph *shows*.

Wherever possible, you want to show.

Think about the first time you saw *Star Wars*. The first half hour of the movie, you weren't really sure where you were or what was happening. Murray the Explainer wasn't in this movie. In fact, nobody in *Star Wars* explains anything. But everything is shown. Seeing how it works is all the explanation you need. Watch. These are spaceships. This one is chasing that one. These are stormtroopers. This is Darth Vader. He's captured the princess. This is a desert planet. These are droids. Jawas capture droids. Jawas sell droids. Luke's uncle buys droids. These are Sand People. This is a bantha. Meet Obi-Wan Kenobi. And finally, after a good forty minutes of chasing R2-D2 and C-3P0, Luke shows us a lightsaber while Obi-Wan explains the Force. (And if you cut that explanation of the Force out of the movie, you would hardly notice it was missing, because the Force is clearly demonstrated in several subsequent scenes.)

In any story, but especially in science fiction and fantasy stories, you have to set the stage right away—and then you have to keep setting it as you go. Every time you move to a new scene, you have to set the stage again.

The best way to set the stage is to show how things work:

> I lowered the faceplate on my suit and turned toward the east. Dawn was racing toward us across the cratered landscape. The bright dazzle of the sun slid up over the horizon and began rising steadily toward zenith. "We'll have to work fast." The commander's voice rang in my headset. "Let's find them before it gets dark again. And remember, no high-bouncing!"

In that one paragraph, there's a lot of information. The narrator is in a space suit. That means he's in a vacuum environment. It's a low-gravity environment, because the commander orders no high-bouncing. Because the sun moves visibly, he's probably on a rotating asteroid. From this paragraph, we don't know how fast it's rotating, but we know it's fast enough that daylight is short. We also know that he's part of a team searching for something. Please notice that *this* paragraph, which explains what the stagesetting paragraph demonstrates, is also *longer*.

To Build a World

*If you don't know, ask. Keep asking until you
think you know. Then keep asking until you're
sure. And then keep asking some more. . . .*

Suppose your story takes place on the moon. Suppose your hero wakes up in a hotel room on the moon. What do you describe?

The first and most obvious difference is gravity. The moon is only one-sixth the size of Earth, so lunar gravity is one-sixth Earth gravity. If you weigh 180 pounds on Earth, you will weigh only 30 pounds on Luna.

That means that every description of someone walking, sitting, running, swimming, pouring a liquid, climbing a ladder, going downstairs, getting up quickly, dropping something, or any other physical activity that we take for granted on Earth, must be *adjusted* for lunar gravity. On the moon, people don't run, they bounce—if you've ever seen the videos of the lunar astronauts, then you've seen their peculiar hop-skip method of bounding across the lunar surface. Imagine how high they'd be bouncing if they weren't wearing 300 pounds of space suit.

But if that's the only aspect of lunar life you include in your story, you're missing all the rest—and if you leave it out, your audience won't feel that you've given them the experience of living on the moon.

If your hero looks out the window, what does he see? You can tell us that he sees the lunar surface, all silvery gray and studded with craters, and that's a familiar view. You can tell us that he sees a crescent Earth low on the horizon—that will tell the astute reader that your hero is somewhere near the far side, and that folks on the Earth are probably seeing a much fuller moon. You can tell us that everything is dark, and we'll know we're somewhere in the middle of a long lunar night—two weeks long. You can tell us that this is a lonely lunar outpost and life is harsh, and we'll believe it.

Now suppose your hero looks out the window and sees a lake and grass and a distant forest of tall green trees, all surrounded by high gray hills, and a bright blue ceiling overhead, then the reader knows he's probably inside a lunar dome—a crater roofed over and filled with air. That's good too. But you can no longer tell us that this is a lonely lunar outpost, because a dome with a park in it suggests a high level of applied technology.

Indeed, everything you add to the dome tells us more about the civilization that built it. This is where you have to start asking yourself questions. Where did the air and water come from? Was it shipped up from Earth? That's hard to believe. Get out your calculator and compute how much air it takes to fill a domed-over crater a couple of miles across. How many tanks of air will have to be shipped from the Earth to the moon? How much will that cost? Who will pay for that? About the time you do that math, you get one of those *fuhgeddaboudit* numbers.

So does that mean you can't have a domed-over crater in your story? No. You can. You just need to know where the air and water is coming from.

As it happens, if you heat lunar rocks hot enough, you can extract oxygen from them. Or if you dig up ice from the lunar north and south poles, you have water that you can electrolyze to produce oxygen and hydrogen as well.

But when you tell the reader that's where the air and

water came from, then you are also telling the reader that there are industrial stations at one or both of the lunar poles to extract the ice, and cost-effective ways of transporting the water and air to your domed city. That *also* implies a lunar society to support those facilities—you'll probably have farms to grow lunar crops. And if you have lunar farms, then that sets up a whole other set of questions too.

Nitrogen, for instance. If you have lunar domes, they won't be filled with pure oxygen. You'll need nitrogen in the atmosphere—a lot of it. You'll also need nitrogen as fertilizer for the crops in your farms—a lot of it. And that means you'll need ammonia, as much as you can import if you can't find any on the moon. There's another problem to solve. You'll probably have to import it from the rings of Saturn. It might be cheaper than lifting it out of the Earth's gravity well. You can make that part of your story, and your reader will be impressed with the depth of your ability to address the issues of technology.

If you're going to have lunar farms, then what kinds of animals will you raise? It might not be practical to take cows to the moon, but you can certainly have chickens and rabbits—and they'll probably grow a lot bigger on the moon. Lunar rabbits might be able to leap thirty or forty feet high. And lunar chickens might even fly, even with their stubby, not-very-aerodynamic wings. But you won't have chickens and rabbits on the moon *unless* you have lunar farms to grow the feed for them.

But all of this technology implies an awful lot of cargo traveling hither and yon all over the moon. If the ice is at the poles and your lunar dome is at the equator (because that's where your launch catapult has to be), then you've got 1666 kilometers of lunar surface between the polar stations and the city under the dome. How are you transporting everything from here to there and back again?

It isn't cost-effective to ship everything on a Kubrick moonbus. Until you can manufacture rocket fuel on the moon, it all has to be imported. And even though the much lighter lunar gravity means you'll use much less fuel per trip, the cost of delivering that fuel to Luna in the first place could be prohibitive. Is there a cheaper way of transporting cargo across the lunar surface?

A lunar train? Who's going to build 1666 kilometers of track in a space suit? While it's an exciting idea, it's just not cost-effective. (Well, maybe robots could do it, but again, that implies a whole other technology and supporting industry.)

Then how about lunar roads and lunar trucks? This is a good idea for short hauls. But again, it's still not cheap enough. You still have to mark the road and bulldoze it. You still have to supply the trucks with fuel and air and water. And even though you can build a truck to carry large amounts of cargo, you need a lot of trucks (and a lot of mechanics) to keep that pipeline running.

Pipeline? Hmm, there's an idea. What kind of pipeline could we build that's cheap to construct, easy to maintain, and lets us move lots of cargo? How about an aerial tramway? Remember the old Skyway ride at Disneyland—all those little buckets hanging from cables, traveling from Fantasyland to Tomorrowland and back again? What if you put up tall towers every ten miles and string cables? What if you ran cargo pods along those cables? You wouldn't have to build roads or lay tracks. You can run branches of your lunar railroad almost anywhere on the moon, so no settlement is ever out of touch. And the electricity to power the system is free; you can put up solar panels on every tower and pipe electricity along the cables to wherever you need it, dayside or night. (The job of constructing those panels, however, is another cost problem.

A lot of water is needed for fabrication.) But yes, an aerial tramway is a believable piece of technology for a growing lunar civilization.

But don't just tell us about the lunar railroad—show it. Use it as part of your story. If someone takes a trip from Armstrong Station to Gagarin Dome, have her get on the train and ride it for a couple of hours. You can then, *as part of the story*, tell us about the train, the cargo it carries from Armstrong to Gagarin, what the scenery looks like as we cross from night into day, and even where the chicken in the sandwich comes from; and all of that is part of setting the stage for your character.

But wait—there's more! Why do you have a city in a domed crater anyway? Is it practical? Well, yes and no. Isn't it a colossal waste of space and resources? Probably. But maybe not.

Suppose your lunar civilization uses air and water as the currency for barter. Let's say one lunar dollar is worth one liter of water. Where does the lunar bank store it? Your polar factories will continue to mine water as long as they can. Where do you put the water and air they produce? Storage tanks? Why not in a big reservoir? Put a dome over a crater and you have the perfect place to store air and water. And as a side benefit, you also have a place to plant grass and trees and crops. And best of all, you end up with a park for people to play in. Build houses and businesses, shops and factories on the inner walls of the crater, and everybody has a marvelous view of the valley below.

So if your hero opens a window and looks out onto a forest across the bottom of a lunar dome—you're also telling the reader that there's a high level of technology behind the construction and maintenance of that society.[5]

---

[5] *Bouncing Off the Moon*, by David Gerrold (Tor Books, 2001).

Remember, no piece of technology ever exists independent of the world that built it. A television needs a television industry to make programs; an airplane needs an airline-service industry to supply passengers, fuel, air traffic controllers, in-flight meals and movies, and flight attendants; a cell phone only works because there's a telephone network for it to connect to. A train needs not only places to go but reasons to go there—important enough to justify the building of trains and the laying of tracks and the service and maintenance of all the different parts of the system.

Building a world is a lot like playing with a set of Lego bricks. You can put them together any way you want but the nature of those little plastic bricks makes some constructions easier than others. The same is true of the building blocks of the physical universe.

Detailing the
World

Planets are not "Earthlike."
Some writers are lazy.

Suppose your story takes place on a different world, circling a distant star.

Your audience wants to see how that world works. They want more than scenery; they want *insight*.

Compare these two paragraphs:

> The Regency Starship, *Akhbar*, peeled itself out of *P-space* with a mechanical shudder that left everyone's fillings ringing painfully. Captain Maribe coaxed the vessel into a parking orbit around a small brown world and ordered the landing boat made ready. "We need a new quantum-dehydrolator, or we'll never make it to the galactic core," she announced to her worried passengers. "The via-scanners detect a wide range of life forms. It could be dangerous. I'll take the landing party down myself. I need three volunteers."

> The *LS-1187* decelerated smoothly through the last hours of approach. Per the mission plan, they came up from below the plane of the ecliptic, releasing high-resolution probes at regular intervals. As they deceler-

ated, the probes raced ahead; the planet's gravity pulled all of them around into tight polar orbits. The starship came in last, keeping its orbit high, while the satellites fired their boosters and maneuvered into lower and faster trajectories. As the world turned beneath, the starship and its remote eyes mapped the alien terrain; in less than two circuits, they would have a detailed atlas. If the enemy had installations here, Commander Korie needed to know. If it became necessary to withdraw quickly, he wanted to have options, and that required accurate information.

Which paragraph gives you a better sense of the mechanics and procedures of space travel? Which one suggests that the author is writing from personal experience?

The first paragraph suggests a starship built like an old bus. If these folks have the technology to build faster-than-light (FTL) starships, how come they're still putting metal fillings in their teeth? The second paragraph shows enough awareness of orbital mechanics, satellite technology, and strategic planning to give a flavor of expertise. The first paragraph has some very silly (and ultimately meaningless) technobabble. The technical term for this is *bolognium*. The second paragraph has no *bolognium*, no made-up words at all; whatever superior technology exists in this story, it is present only by implication.

Science fiction requires research. (So does fantasy, although not necessarily the same kind.) When you design a planet, you start first by designing the whole star system. First, decide on the star. Some kinds of stars are impractical for viable planets; they're either too big or too old or too dangerous. You're going to have to spend some time with a couple of good resources to find out the difference between a white dwarf and a red giant. (In a fantasy novel, a white dwarf and a red giant are probably the best of buddies and will have many wonderful adventures together.)

You can postulate a star that's much like our own friendly Sol, but it can't be *exactly* like it. A believable star could be bigger and older, and maybe has more orange and red in its spectrum. If it's smaller, it's probably white or blue in color. This will affect what it looks like from the surface of the world you're designing.

The planet you create is probably about 160 million kilometers from its sun, farther if the sun is bigger, closer if the sun is smaller. If people are to be comfortable there, it has to exist in that realm of temperatures in which human life can survive with a minimum of mechanical assistance.

One of the most important decisions will be the nature of the planet's orbit. How long does it take to circle its star? How long is its year? Is the orbit circular or elliptical? Is it in the plane of the ecliptic? Does it tilt on its axis? If so, how severe is the tilt? Earth is tilted only 23.5°, but this is sufficient to provide four distinct seasons a year. What happens to your world and its seasons if the tilt is even more severe? What kind of seasons will it have if the orbit is elliptical? And if the orbit tilts out of the plane of the ecliptic, what kind of meteoric bombardment will it experience?

How long is the planet's day? Twenty hours? Thirty-six hours? Two weeks? A month? What does this do to the surface temperatures? Luna has a day that is four weeks long, two weeks of light and two weeks of dark. This means that temperatures are 160° above zero at high noon, and 40° below zero at midnight. (And that's *without* an atmosphere.)

By the way, does your planet have moons? How many? How big? What do they look like from the ground?

And how much water does this planet have? Does it have

large oceans like Earth? If not, where's the water? Water is necessary for life. What's the weather like? The warmer the oceans are, the more severe the hurricanes become. The more extreme the temperature conditions, the worse the winds.

Does your planet have a lot of iron or nickel in its core? If it does, that affects both gravity and magnetism. If your planet doesn't have much heavy metal in its composition, it can be larger than Earth and still have less gravity. But it won't have enough magnetic field to turn a compass north, let alone supply the materials for heavy industry. That will affect the development of technology, navigation, shipping, and all the cultural developments that follow. Scientific thinking might have a much harder time gaining a foothold. This would be a good planet for a fantasy.

Most important, what kind of atmosphere does your planet have? Be careful how you answer.

See, there's this thing called "the oxygen cycle. . . ."

Oxygen is made by plants—and if you have plants, you also have animals. Because plants can't exist without animals, and vice versa. The two need each other to exist. (And insects too, but that's a different discussion.)

If your planet has water, it will almost certainly have life. Life is almost inevitable where water is available. But if the planet has no water, it cannot have life. And if it has no life, it will have very little free oxygen.

Of course, this assumes life based on CHON—carbon, hydrogen, oxygen, and nitrogen. If you want to create life that is not based on CHON, you can do that too. You can postulate methane-breathing, silicon-based life forms, if you want—but you'll have to present that biochemistry as a believable possibility, and that'll be even harder than good old CHON. You'll probably need degrees in chemistry and biology.

And then there's the whole issue of ecology. . . .

Predators need prey. Everything eats, everything gets eaten. Nothing dies of old age in nature. Sunlight feeds the plants, the plants feed the insects and the animals; the animals drop dung and feed the microbes which turn the dung into fertilizer which feeds the plants; the animals die and feed the insects. Round and round it goes. Life is fecund. (There's an understatement.)

On Earth, the complex web of interrelationships between species is vast beyond comprehension; it will likely be the same on any other worlds we discover. Your audience knows this; they will expect you to acknowledge the possibilities, even if you don't answer all the questions:

> The thing is—Outbeyond didn't *look* as dreadful as Boynton had made it sound.
>
> The planet is in a slightly elliptical orbit, not quite in the plane of the ecliptic, so it's the oddball in the system. Its orbit isn't Earthlike, but it's almost. Everything about the planet is *almost*. Twice a year, it's about ten million miles closer to its sun than Earth is to Sol, and twice a year it's about twenty million miles farther away. This means that there are 8 seasons in a year. Each season is only two months long and the year has 16 months.
>
> What all this means is that Outbeyond's equatorial regions are unlivable. Temperatures range from 110 degrees in winter to 180 degrees in summer. The temperate zones are only 20 degrees cooler. The poles are 50-100 degrees cooler than the equator, depending on season. There's some snow and ice, but only at higher elevations.
>
> —Oh yeah, most of the mountains are volcanoes, because the planet's weird shape puts a lot of stress

on the tectonic plates. Every so often, they all go off at once, dumping gigatons of soot into the atmosphere, enough to cause widespread planetary cooling—sometimes as long as a decade or two.

Outbeyond doesn't have as much water as Earth, but it's more evenly distributed in a lot of skinny seas and large lakes, all interconnected and sort of spiraling outward from the poles. Because of the temperature differences between the poles and the equator, and the heat stored in the oceans, the weather is ferocious. Tornadoes on the flatlands, scalding super-hurricanes on the seas, monsoons that sweep across the continents, and hot raging dust storms from the equator scourging all the way to what we would call the temperate (ha ha) zones.

Despite all this, there's life. Of a sort.

Outbeyond is kind of like what Earth would have been if the comet hadn't smacked into Yucatan 65 million years ago and wiped out all the dinosaurs, giving all the egg-sucking little therapsids a chance to evolve into mammals and hominids and eventually people. So there are still dinosaurs on this planet. Well, things *like* dinosaurs, but not really, because they're sort of mammalian too. And forests. Huge forests. Trees as tall as skyscrapers. Thick jungles, filled with all kinds of snakes and lizards and flying things and crawling things and buzzing things and biting things. And more stuff like that underwater too, but none of it catalogued yet.

But the important thing is that Outbeyond can support *human* life too. You can actually go outside without a mask and not fall immediately to the ground, clutching your throat, gasping for breath, as blood pours out of your ears and nose, and vomit spews out of your mouth. Outbeyond has enough oxygen in its atmosphere that humans can actually *breathe* it. The problem is that it has *too much* oxygen in its atmosphere, which means that things burn a lot faster, so fire is a lot more dangerous.

Outbeyond's oceans aren't as salty as on Earth. Probably because the twice-yearly dust monsoon season scours right down to the bottom of the seas and dredges them deeper, pouring lots of dust into the upper atmosphere, where it circles around until it settles out over the equator to fuel the raging hot dust storms; so a lot of the salt is in the equatorial regions.

But the equatorial dust storms pick up just as much and drop it back into the oceans, and that feeds the proto-plankton and that means food for the little fish in the sea that the bigger fish eat. There are all kinds of things in the ocean, and almost all of them are constantly migrating with the currents to avoid the seasonal extremes.

The more we looked at the pictures, the more we started to think that maybe it wasn't going to be as hard as Boynton suggested. Some of those pictures were awfully tempting.

Because the star was so bright, all the colors were more intense, so when they showed the pictures of all the flowers, with blossoms bigger than a person's head, both Mom and Bev gasped. The bad news was that the scientist standing next to the flowers—a guy named Guiltinan—was holding his nose and shaking his head and making a dreadful face. The flowers were pretty enough to look at, but according to the narrator, they made a dreadful smell, worse than a rotting corpse. So springtime was a good time to stay inside. When whole fields of plants opened up, the smells could carry on the wind for hundreds of kilometers.

The example above is taken from chapter three of a novel called *Leaping to the Stars*.[6] The narrator is a thirteen-year-old boy named Chigger. He and his family have to choose from several different colony worlds, including Outbeyond.

Sometimes there's no escaping it, you have to drop a big lump of exposition into the story. As much as you want to show and demonstrate, sometimes you have to stop and tell—otherwise the readers won't know where the characters are going or why they're going there. Sometimes you can sneak the exposition in, a little at a time—and sometimes you can't.

If you do have to tell it all at once, you can make the telling interesting by adding personal asides as you go. In the paragraphs above, notice how Chigger explains things in his own voice? He gives you the flavor of the Outbeyond *as he perceives it*. This isn't accidental. Everything in the story has to be seen through the hero's eyes. His perceptions are the voice of the book.

---

[6] A sequel to *Bouncing Off the Moon*, by the same author. Ahem. (See the chapter on shameless self-promotion.)

Building Aliens

*Alien means different. It does not mean
pointed ears, a wrinkly forehead, or a
crinkled nose. It means different!*

After you've built your alien world, you have to populate it.

Dr. Jack Cohen, a British biologist and author of many books on reproduction, biology, and evolution, has occasionally offered his services to various science fiction authors to assist in the construction of alien ecologies. He advised Anne McCaffrey on the dragons of Pern; he advised Larry Niven, Jerry Pournelle, and Steven Barnes on the samlons and "beowulfs" in *The Legacy of Heorot*; and he gave me yeoman service, more than once, in the construction of the Chtorran ecology in my own, *War Against the Chtorr*.

Dr. Cohen also appears occasionally at the World Science Fiction convention to give a slide-show presentation on alien ecologies. His rule is simple, "If you can show me a Terran analog for this behavior, I'll believe it."

If you postulate an alien species where the newborn infants eat their parents . . . well, there are Terran insect species that do that, so you have evidence that it can happen in nature. If you suggest a ribbon-like creature that moves through the air by rippling its body in a perfect sine wave, Dr. Cohen will believe that too; there's a creature that lives in the sea that does exactly that. You can even postulate a creature that splits into two separate creatures for reproductive purposes—we have Terran symbioses that work like that. There are species of fish and lizards that change

sex if there are not enough available partners of the opposite sex. There are twenty-seven species of reptiles that have
no male members at all and have to reproduce parthenoge-
netically.[7] There is a species of fly that develops into two
very different forms, depending on its environment; it looks
like two totally different species.[8]

On the other hand, if you postulate a species of alien
that takes its head off at night so the body can go
feed . . . well, Dr. Cohen is going to have a bit of trouble
with that. You don't find that on Earth. (You'd have to
argue that this is a symbiotic relationship, and you'd have
to demonstrate that both organisms benefit from the relationship. Otherwise, why should the body come back?)

The more you know of the great variety of organisms
found on this planet, the more you know what might be
possible on other planets. As convenient as it is to say,
"Captain, sensors indicate a race of silicon-based, methane
breathers," that particular assertion creates many *more*
problems than it solves.

The counterarguments to the above—and I have heard
them offered more than once from folks who don't get the
point—are that "Dr. Cohen doesn't know everything," and
"Just because it doesn't happen on Earth doesn't mean it
can't happen somewhere else." Both of those assertions are
true, but they don't really address the issue.

You want to achieve *believability*. You want your audience
to believe in your aliens. An audience will believe in a nine-
foot-tall creature with superdangerous acid flowing through
its veins; they'll believe in a gigantic hairy elephant living on
a desert planet where nothing grows that it can eat; and they'll

---

[7]—most well-known is the whiptail lizard (*Discover* magazine, April 1987).
[8] At one point, I had considered every creature in the Chtorran ecology having identical
DNA. They were all the same creature, but expressing itself in different forms and
using different parts of the genetic sequence. It's still a possibility. . . .

even believe in a thousand-year-old, walking baseball glove that eats chocolate-covered peanut-butter pellets and can make things fly by the power of its mind. They'll believe these things for about two hours at a time *because they want to believe them*—but only so long as the creator establishes an internally consistent system of logic.

If you want to build an interesting alien species, you should start with these questions:

- What is the home planet like? (At the poles, at the equator, in the temperate regions?)
- How did this species evolve? What did they evolve *from?*
- How does this species reproduce? Do they have a limited mating season? What kind of mating rituals do they have? How many sexes participate?
- Do they lay eggs or give live birth? What are the offspring like? What kind of life cycles do the offspring pass through? What kind of physical and mental transformations do they experience in the process of reproduction, birth, and growth?
- What does this species eat? How do they feed? What kind of relationship do they have with their food? (Think about it.)
- What other species do they have ecological partnerships with? What do they prey on? What preys on them?
- How long do the members of this race live? How fast does time pass for them?
- How are their physical bodies shaped by the environment in which they live? (What kind of gravity, sunlight, weather, humidity, etc., are they adapted to?)
- What kind of technology (if any) does this race have? How do they use it?

- What religious rituals do they have? What is the underlying philosophy of their civilization? Why? How does this serve them? How does it *not* serve them?
- How do they communicate? What is interesting or special about their language?
- What is the psychology of this alien race?

The last question deserves particular attention. Most of what you tell the reader about your aliens will serve as scenery—but how they think will determine how they act. That's what makes them *alien*. They think *different*.

For instance, suppose you have a species that only achieves intelligence when multiple individuals pool their thinking ability? Such a species would not recognize individual human beings as intelligent. And human beings would be puzzled how such a species could achieve intelligent behaviors when all of the individual members are not. The inability to recognize the different shapes of each other's intelligence would lead to massive misunderstandings.

Or suppose you have a (very politically incorrect) species where only the males are intelligent. The females are kept in pens like herd animals and used only for breeding. Humans couldn't send female ambassadors to such a world without it being an insult. And the leaders of that race might not consider humans an intelligent species at all if the males were no smarter than the females.

How about a symbiotic partnership between two species? The "head" has evolved to the point where it cannot feed itself; it has to live like a parasite off the labor of the "body." The body needs the intelligence of the head so it can find food. Both head and body can survive apart for a while, but neither can survive for long without the cooperation of the other. Such a partnership might lend itself to body-swapping by heads. What kind of psychology would that create? If you could change your body conveniently, then young strong bodies would be in demand, and old feeble ones would be discarded. Would bodies reject some kinds of heads as being too aggressive or too weak? Would heads be able to prolong their lives by switching to younger bodies? Would rich heads have a stable of bodies? Would this symbiotic race consider humans to be a primitive and unevolved form?

Consider a race where the individual member cycles through different forms as it grows. At various ages, it functions as an egg incubator, a female, a male, an alpha, and a patriarch. In that society, the individual's sexual identity would be congruent with its age *and status*. Because every citizen would eventually experience all the sexual roles, there would be no permanent differentiation of gender as an identifier. Sex would be a function of age, not birth; but the society would still have a class- and age-based caste system. If humans contacted such a species, they would consider us evolutionarily retarded; they would see us as stuck in our life-phases, and therefore *insane*.

Now compare these idea-seeds with the kinds of aliens you see on television. . . .

Right.

It is insufficient for aliens to be modeled after humans, with two eyes, a nose, and a mouth. Ferengi ears or a Klingon forehead is not *alien*—it's *makeup*. Vulcan stoicism is about as alien as a trip to the autism ward.[9] Romulans are no more alien than feudal Japan.

Modeling alien behavior on human traits is a convenient shortcut. It's also lousy science fiction.

It is, however, terrific fantasy. . . .

---

[9] In fact, you're likely to find far more *alien* thinking in the average psychotic than you will find in the average television alien. I know this sounds hard to believe, but television writers and producers aren't psychotic *enough*.

Believability

I think, therefore I doubt.

Beware the "refrigerator door" question! Ever notice how sometimes you go to a movie and you see what you think is a terrific picture? You have a marvelous time; afterward, you go out for coffee and sit around chatting with your friends about what a wonderful movie you've just seen. Finally you head for home; later that night you decide to have a little snack, and just as you open the refrigerator door, the question hits you smack in the face: *Hey! If E.T. could fly at the end of the movie to save himself and Elliott, why the hell didn't he fly away at the beginning of the movie when they were first chasing him?*[10] And you stand there in front of the open refrigerator, your snack forgotten, realizing you've been conned and cheated, while the ice cream melts in your hand.

Sometimes the refrigerator door question reaches out of the screen and bites you even as the dialogue is still falling out of the actors' mouths. How come in the movie *Independence Day*, Earth scientists were immediately able to decode the operating system and data files of an alien computer system? Most of us have enough trouble running the computer systems we do know. And if Han Solo can make the Kessel Run in less than twelve parsecs, why doesn't he know that a parsec is a measure of distance, not time?

---

[10] This one is easy to answer. He didn't have a bicycle. . . .

Yes, you can postulate something that violates our experience of the way the world works; just know that you're inventing a special form of *bolognium*.

The term comes from Larry Niven, author of *Ringworld*, one of the best science fiction novels of the twentieth century. In *Ringworld*, Niven postulated a gigantic ring circling a star. It had the surface area of millions of planets, and trillions of beings lived on it. In order to construct this massive object, Niven postulated "scrith," a substance strong enough to build a ring 180 million miles in diameter. There is no such substance in the known universe, but Niven needed it for his story. So he invented it. It was pure unadulterated *bolognium*. Absolutely necessary for the story—and absolutely preposterous by the known laws of physics.

In that same story, Niven also postulated a character named Teela Brown, who was the result of seven consecutive generations of winners of the breeding lottery. She had been "bred for luck." This is another form of *bolognium*—an outlandish power or ability, presently unknown. Obviously, we don't know if it's possible to breed for luckiness, but Niven needed it for the resolution of his story—he needed to make an impossible chain of events look inevitable. The story included a couple of other kinds of *bolognium* as well, including stasis fields and slaver weapons and several very interesting species of aliens.

Niven says that there is a limited amount of *bolognium* a writer can put into a story. A good science fiction story can sustain one piece of *bolognium* quite well. Stories with two pieces of *bolognium* require significant skill in juggling and should not be attempted by beginners. Three pieces of *bolognium* represent critical mass, and no one less than a grand master should attempt such a challenge. Stories with four or more pieces of *bolognium* are called "fantasies."

The trick with *bolognium* is to handle it as if it's a toxic material. Wear protective gear and handle it with tongs, or better yet, work through robotic arms. If you want the reader to believe something impossible, you have to find a way to connect it to something the reader already knows. One of the best examples of this is the discussion of how to breed a new generation of dinosaurs in *Jurassic Park* (either the book or the film). Even though common sense tells us that it's impossible for the genetic material of dinosaurs to have survived for sixty-five million years, the author's careful discussion of how the DNA can be retrieved from the bodies of mosquitoes sealed in ancient amber is just convincing enough to energize our desire to *believe*.

When a storyteller invents a colossal whopper—a tale so tall it needs an express elevator—he needs to seduce the reader's cooperation in creating believability. The author does that by grounding the story in the reality of the reader's own experience. If you want to lend believability to an outrageous idea, you surround it with a whole bunch of other things that *feel* believable. Think of your story as a colossal lie; the trick in selling a lie is to surround it with so much truth that the listener believes the lie is also true.

Alfred Bester wrote what many consider the greatest science fiction novel of all time, *The Stars My Destination*. It was predicated on one single piece of *bolognium*—that human beings have an inherent psychokinetic ability to teleport through space (and later, time). He called this skill "jaunting." To make it believable, he did a brief history of how the skill was accidentally discovered when a scientist jaunted himself out of a certain-death situation—and how other scientists tested for the existence of the ability to jaunt. He took the preposterous and surrounded it with the scientific method and examined how it would work. He created specific limits and rules. (For instance, you couldn't jaunt to any place you'd never been, because you needed a mental target.)

Do not make the *Star Trek* mistake. Do not confuse technobabble with science.

How many times have you had the experience of watching an episode of a science fiction television show where the problem was solved by someone turning up the knob on the double-talk generator? Did you feel frustrated and cheated? You should. That's not science fiction—that's desperation on the part of an incompetent writer.

> DATA
> It's life, Captain, but not as we know it. A creature of pure energy.

> GEORDI
> (concerned)
> I can't give you any more power, Cap'n. The creature has transmogrified the dilithium volatizers and the blabberfax can't handle the increase in plaso-dimensional discoordination stress. We'll have to immobilize the greezinchokker or the ship will be narfled into quiblets!

> PICARD
> I know you can do it, Mr. LaForge! Go to Warp 11!

> WESLEY
> Captain! I have an idea! If we cross-polarize the dibbletizer, just by switching these two colored wires, we can reinvent transwarp capability and achieve speeds

as high as Warp 37 at half the power. Gosh,
why didn't some grown-up think of this
already? No wonder you need a fifteen-
year-old supergenius on this ship!

                    Q
              (to himself)
With all my superpowers, why am I wasting my time on these chimpanzees?

In 1966, when *Star Trek* first came on the air, Gene
Roddenberry established a very simple rule: "If I won't
believe it on the bridge of the battleship *Iowa*, I won't believe it on the bridge of the starship *Enterprise.*"

If only the subsequent inheritors of the *Star Trek* tradition had listened. . . .

Fantasy Worlds

*Even when you think there's nothing
more to discover, keep asking.*

Now let's do that again, this time with a fantasy world.

Some fantasies are gentle, others are more detailed, and some are positively baroque. Some are rooted in history, and some are firmly grounded in thin air. But no matter how fantastic the initial premise, you are obligated to develop the world as rigorously as if you were describing an actual physical location. As with science fiction, the same strict principles of logic apply.

Suppose, for example, you want to tell a rousing adventure yarn that takes place in Atlantis, the fabled lost continent that sank beneath the sea. You are obligated to be consistent with historical fact, at least to the extent that the reader is familiar with it.

One of the first things you will have to decide is where Atlantis could be found on the ancient maps. Although all we know about Atlantis is a brief description in Plato's writings, quite a few books (of varying degrees of scholarship and research) have been published on the subject. Because your audience will be those who are interested in lost continents, you can expect them to have some familiarity with the various theories, both serious and crackpot. So you'll have to be consistent with what they know . . . or you'll have to come up with a new extrapolation even more convincing.

Many scholars think Atlantis might have existed somewhere in the Mediterranean, and they point to various sunken islands that seem to match Plato's description of the lost world. Others have said that the entire Mediterranean was once a dry valley—until the ocean broke through at Gibraltar and flooded the region. Whichever theory you subscribe to, you'll need to determine a location for your story, and you'll have to keep your descriptions consistent with what we know of ancient times.

For instance, the Sahara was once a vast savanna, a land of lush grass and forest, teeming with wildlife—until the Roman Empire stripped the land of trees and exported the animals to their arenas. They didn't see the damage they were doing because it was occurring over generations. They wanted the wood for their ships and their cities, so they took it without regard for the future—and they left behind a legacy of sand. The deserts of North Africa are man-made, but they would not have existed in the time of Atlantis, at least not on the scale we now know.

This is information that some of your readers might already know—it is also information that could surprise and delight those who have not heard this before. In either case, including it enriches the depth of your story's environment. The background of your story is more than just so much painted scenery. It's a setting that people interact with.

Try another:

Suppose you're telling a story in which your hero travels to the land of Faerie to bring King Oberon the gift of a virgin's tear wrapped in a white rose petal. For the purposes of your narrative, you want Oberon's realm to be mysterious and even a bit dangerous. You need it to be recognizably magical—you need it to be specifically *different*.

So you think for a bit. It seems to you that the most magical time of day is twilight, so you decide that the kingdom of Faerie is a twilight realm—neither day nor night.

The landscape is dark and shadowy, but the sky still has light seeping through it. At the edge of your vision, there are glitters in the air—not fireflies; it's the giggling of pixies, sparkling as they dance away out of sight.

Oberon's palace is a high silken tent, seemingly made of glistening spider webs. The king and queen of Faerie sit on thrones of dandelion and rose. When they speak, you hear silver bells. The scent of lilac in moonlight comes to you.

The King of Faerie looks at you with wisdom as well as amusement. And no small amount of hostility. Foolish humans are cutting down the trees, destroying the homes of the forest folk. Foolish humans are destroying the magic in the world. Why should any human ask the mercy of the old people of the world, let alone a favor?

Yes, OK—you decide that works for your story. It's a magical mood, subtle yet dangerous, and consistent with the traditional portrayal of the land of Faerie. So now you know where your hero is going—but how does he get there?

Does he just walk into the forest? That's the traditional method, and nobody would fault you for writing it that way; but let's suppose you want to go beyond the traditional. You want to show how a human travels from the bright sunlight of the mortal realm to the twilight dreamscape of Faerie.

And here is where we begin to discover the underlying logic that your story requires. If you have decided that the land of Faerie is a dreamscape, then it cannot have a specific physical location. Nevertheless, it has to be accessible to your hero, and the method of access has to be believable within the logic of the story.

So perhaps you decide to create a bit of lore: *To reach the realm of Faerie, you must travel west until twilight.*

Hmm. You think about that for a bit—what happens if you're traveling west and you don't want to end up in the land of Faerie? Stop before twilight? Maybe it would be better to make the rule: *To reach the realm of Faerie, travel west at twilight*. Or maybe: *West at twilight, when the moon is full*. That might work—especially if magic is strongest under the full moon.

Or maybe: *West until you get there*. If you're a wizard, three steps west should be sufficient. And if you have little or no belief in magic at all, you can travel west forever and never get there. So perhaps the magical beliefs and abilities of the traveler are part of the equation.

Notice that this is world-building just as rigorous as you would do for a science fiction novel. Whatever rules you set, you're going to be stuck with them until the last page of the story, so you have to be careful.

So . . . your hero travels west for three days. And as twilight creeps across the world at the end of the third day, the forest changes around him. The air turns still, and the color seeps from the sky, and the sounds of the birds and the insects fade away, replaced by the distant sound of silvery bells. . . .

That works. That establishes that you reach the realm of Faerie when you're ready to step into it—and that creates it in the reader's mind as a dream reality, sideways to the land of flesh and bone.

But maybe that doesn't work for your story . . .

Suppose you've written that the Lord of Blackmark Castle has taken grievous offense at a puckish prank. Having received no apology from Oberon, he declares war on the realm of the Old Folke. If that's your story, then Faerie has to exist as a specific physical location. Otherwise, his army could travel west forever, and never arrive at Faerie. Oberon wouldn't grant them access.

So to suit the needs of your story, you have to say that Faerie is a specific land, far to the west, shrouded in perpetual twilight.

—and the minute you make that decision, you've automatically created a whole landscape, one filled with every bit as much detail as the lunar civilization you created when your science fiction hero opened a window and looked out onto a domed-over crater with a forest growing in it, because if you've postulated a realm of magic and a realm of *not*-magic, then the reader wants to know: *What lies between the two realms?*

What's the dividing line? Is it a simple low wall that the hero steps over and he's there? On one side, spells and charms work; on the other side, they don't.

Or perhaps there's a wall of forbidding mountains, high and impenetrable; you can only enter the kingdom of magic across a narrow bridge over a deep chasm where the winds howl like ghosts.

Or maybe the transition is more gradual. The farther west the hero proceeds, the more magical the world becomes. Perhaps there are borderlands where neither magic nor mortality rule—and the hero must cross through the unformed terrain to reach the realm of Faerie. Now you must consider, *what will you find in the borderlands? What will the borderlands look like? Who lives there?* Perhaps the land itself is twisted and unreal, with the scenery shifting and changing as the winds of magic blow. Perhaps the things that live there are half-breeds of mortal and magic. They cannot survive too long in either realm.

Notice again, whatever you build, there must be an underlying logic to your construction. Some of this you will invent consciously to fit the needs of your story, and some of it will fall into place because it just *feels* right. (And when things fall into place that way, pat yourself on the back—you're in the flow.)

Stories are about journeys—not always a voyage through a physical landscape, of course, but certainly a trek through the emotional realms of life. Traveling through the terrain, physical or emotional, is the best way to demonstrate how it works. The more different aspects you portray, the more interesting it becomes.

But let's continue on a bit longer. Let's step into one of the bear traps. . . .

If there is a land to the west that is always twilight, what does this suggest about the cosmology of this world? Are we on a planet? Or are we on an endless plain? If we're on a planet, then the only way to have a realm of perpetual twilight is for the planet to have one face always turned toward the sun—and that means that Blackmark Castle is probably a molten puddle anyway. And on the other side, beyond the realm of Faerie twilight, is a realm of perpetual ice. (A Nordic version of Hell perhaps?)

So how do you manage this? The mortal land has a normal progression of days and nights, and a normal sky of stars; but in the land of Faerie, there is no sun or moon—halfway between night and day, the horizons glow and the sky seeps with light; in the forests and meadows, shadows spread veils of mystery. Some readers are going to wonder how you arranged the physics of this. How can an Earthlike world have a habitable domain of perpetual twilight?

The easy way to resolve this is to decide that the laws of reality are different in the realm of magic—the land of Faerie is turned perpendicular to the rest of the universe, and time flows sideways. And most readers will accept that bit of double-talk as a way of lubricating the friction between the mortal world and the magic one. Especially if you're telling a good story.

Fantasy is like a soufflé. It's delicate. You have to treat it with respect. Yes, you can create things that violate the known laws of physics, but when you do, you have to balance them gently atop what the reader already knows about reality *and* fantasy. Look long and hard at what you want to build. If you write what you're willing to believe, it's likely that the audience will believe as well.

Here's an example:

> Erindell moaned in distress. The entire forest roiled with disturbance. The youngtrees swayed in anguish; the bigtrees sobbed, pumping the air up through their columnar throats. The notes were so deep they were felt rather than heard—a pressure in the air that gave the travelers queasy feelings in their bellies. Despite their deafness, the horses stirred uneasily, so much that finally the riders dismounted and blindfolded the steeds to walk them in safety. All around, the rustling of leaves and branches sounded like the howling of a storm, but the air beneath remained still—as if they moved within a bubble of calm.
>
> "What does it mean?" Vellar asked the tree-girl.
>
> She couldn't answer. She was shaking badly, as badly as the forest. She held out a hand to touch the nearest bigtree, then recoiled as if burned. Her face showed suffering, she could barely control herself. "I don't know. Something awful has happened—might still be happening." Overcome, she collapsed sobbing to the ground.
>
> "Say it!" Vellar commanded sharply—and regretted it instantly. The tone of his voice only made the girl howl like the trees. But he was a prince, he was used to giving orders, and the strange ways of the tree people frustrated and annoyed him. An idea came to

him; he pulled off his heavy cloak and wrapped it around the girl, as if it would shield her somewhat. "Does this help?" he asked.

She nodded and managed to gasp. "Thank you."

"Is it a battle?" he asked. She shook her head. Vellar tried to think what might have panicked the trees. "Is it a forest fire?" he asked. "Or swarms of locusts?"

"Worse! Much worse! I've never felt such madness. The smell of dreadful death is in the wind—somewhere trees are dying violently. And Erindell is screaming in sympathy as well as fear." She looked as if she wanted to bolt herself. "We have to get away from here—" she tried to insist.

Vellar grabbed her arm. "Stay with us," he commanded.

Something in the distance crashed. All the travelers turned as one—just in time to see one of the biggest of the bigtrees come ripping downward, branches tearing as it toppled, all the trees around it screaming. The writhing of the forest became a wild frenzy.

"They're dying!" shrieked the girl. "They're uprooting themselves in panic! It's only going to get worse—"

"We can't go on this way!" shouted the commander of the guard. He pointed. "We have to go back."

Prince Vellar shook his head. He raised his voice to be heard. "No. We will not go back to the gray lands. We lost too many men and horses getting this far. We'll push on to the high country. If we can get above the tree line, where it's calmer, the Mage can send his soul aloft and search the horizons."

"We'll never make it to the high country—" the commander said.

Vellar turned back to the girl. She was struggling in his grasp. "Where is it safe?" he demanded. "Where can we go?"

The girl sank to her knees and dug her fingers into the soft dirt, as if she were taking root—as if she were searching for something. "Deep," she gasped. "As deep as we can get—" She opened her eyes as if she were looking into the next life—a strange expression crossed her face. Her eyes widened, almost bulging out of her skull, but she didn't seem in pain. She crooned low in her throat, as if singing to a distant ear.

Abruptly, she pulled her hands free of the dirt and pointed. "This way!"

Vellar and the others followed her—the Mage, in his hooded cloak and with his mask still shielding his face, the six remaining soldiers in their leather breastplates, the two frightened servants, and the skinny page. Around them, the wailing of the trees had reached deafening proportions. Vellar realized— *too late*—that the girl was leading them straight into the screaming heart of the forest's panic.

Suddenly, ahead—a circle of dead and dying trees—and in the center, a low mound punctuated with pig-sized openings. The tree-girl flattened herself and began crawling forward. "This way, quickly—" She glanced back. "Get down! All of you, get down and crawl!"

"No!" cried Vellar.

"Would you rather die?"

"We can't leave the horses!"

"You have to! They're the price I paid for your lives! Now follow me before it's too late—" She began crawling down into the nearest hole. The Mage was close behind her, gathering his cloak as he dropped to his knees.

"Everyone follow them—" Vellar ordered.

The commander shook his head. "Not me. Not my troops—"

"I order you—"

"No longer!" the captain of the guard cried angrily. "Not one step further. No more lives lost for this madness!"

"Then to hell with you!" said Vellar. He looked to the servants and the page. "And what about you three? Where are your loyalties?" The two servants backed away, eyes wide with fear, but the boy scrambled after the Mage.

Vellar glared angrily at the disloyal soldiers, glanced upward at the reddening sky, then reluctantly dropped to the ground and scrambled into the nest after the page.

The darkness closed in around him. His eyesight disappeared, leaving him with a confusing welter of sounds and smells and uncomfortable feelings. What was that coldness he touched? What was that distant trilling? And what was that sickening odor? The nest smelled bitter and rank.

He crawled down the cramped tunnel with a deepening feeling of despair. How had he ended up here? Had his stupid royal pride finally brought him to disaster? He thrust the thought away. The girl had been right so far. If he'd listened to her sooner, the lives of twelve good men might not have been lost to the sand beasts of the gray lands.

Vellar tumbled out into a cramped chamber, barely larger than a closet. The girl, the Mage, and the boy were arrayed closely around the edges. The Mage had produced a soft light, barely enough to see by. He held a gloved finger to the carved lips of his mask. *Make no sound.*

From above, there came the noise of screams. Men and horses alike—*the price paid for their lives.*

Vellar listened in paralyzed horror. Even after the last scream had stopped, he was sure he could still hear the sounds of death. Perhaps it wasn't death he was hearing, but hideous hunger being sated.

The girl touched his arm; she pointed to a tunnel in the floor of the chamber. "We must go down," she whispered. "The queen wants to meet you. She has never met a *man* before."

Vellar hesitated.

"You will be safe," the girl said. "The queen's daughters are as afraid of us as we are of them. They will not approach. But the queen wants to meet you. It is *not* a request," she added, unsubtly.

Vellar wanted nothing more than to head back up the way he'd come, away from this cramped confining space, away from this terrible encroaching darkness and the dreadful smell of this nest—

Notice, in this fragment of an unpublished work, there's a great deal of exposition presented. It's presented while the characters are on the move, but at the end of the section, you know that the trees are sentient enough to have emotion, emotional enough to be driven mad by the smells of other trees dying. The humans are only passing through; they've never been here before—this is a strange and terrifying place to them.

From the narrative, you know that the Mage's spirit can leave his body and go out searching, but his power appears to have limits. The girl has some kind of relationship with the forest, enough so that she can be its voice for the moment. And finally, even though it's never clearly said, there's no question that the survivors of this scene are climbing into the burrow of a colony of giant insects—termites or ants—and the queen of this colony is not only sentient, but a cruel bargainer indeed. Before we've even met her, she's collected her bloody price. Also, Vellar is of royal blood, but unused to command. He doesn't seem to deal well with anyone. He doesn't even know the girl's name yet. He has not yet matured as a leader. Oh, and by the way, the girl knows more than she's saying.

None of this is explained; *it's all shown through Vellar's eyes*. The reader identifies with Vellar, because the narrative is suffused with his thoughts and feelings—no one else's.

Overall, you should get a sense that this is a consistent and believable ecology, because everything connects to everything else. Giant insects have giant appetites; they kill trees to build their burrows—ahh, they're termites. And something that the insects are doing is driving the forest mad with fear. We don't know what, but we know that the insect burrow is at the heart of the panic. Something is happening within. The same telepathy which allows the girl to understand the moaning of the trees also allows her to mind-speak with the insects. *And the queen wants to meet Vellar!*

If the author succeeds in fitting the pieces together, you won't question them. If the pieces don't fit, you won't believe them. It really is that simple.

Complications

*No problem is ever as big as it
looks. Usually, it's bigger.*

A problem is like a Chinese puzzle box—the kind where
you have to slide open one panel after the other, each
one providing access to the next part of the puzzle. Every
time you solve one part of it, you only reveal the next
part that has to be solved. The more you work on a problem, the more complicated it seems to become. I like to
call this the *polymurphic* progression (i.e. Murphy's Law
polymorphs).

For instance, suppose you decide to cook an omelet for
lunch. You reach for the frying pan and discover that the
handle is loose, so you go looking for a screwdriver—but
the screwdriver isn't in the junk drawer where you left it,
so you go to the hardware store to buy a new screwdriver,
but your credit card is maxed out, so you get in the car
and drive to the ATM to take out some money, but you're
overdrawn in your checking account, so you go digging
through the parking meter money in the ashtray to see if
you have the $2.49 in change, only you cut your finger on
the metal edge and have to spend $1.99 on Band-Aids,
and by the time you've staunched the bleeding, you're not
hungry anymore—and if you work this right, you can go
all day without eating, except that Mom is coming over
and . . . never mind, you get the idea. Nothing is easy.

What's really happening here is that the problem is un-
raveling into all its component parts. You are discovering

all the details of the situation that make it a problem.

The same is true of a science fiction or fantasy story. A situation has details, most of which are boring—but some of which are illuminating.

Suppose, for example, that your hero is a wandering knight who has set out to find the Amulet of Yendor. It turns out that the amulet is held by the gray wizard who lives in the castle of Moloch, and the only way to get into the castle of Moloch is to ring a silver bell of opening, light the candles of enlightenment (of course), and read a spell from the great book of enchantments. (And don't forget that an occasional whack with the axe of contrition will make any enemies sorry they got in the way.) But to get the silver bell of opening, the knight must first slay the demon lord Ixoth, who has stolen Merlin's magic mirror; only when he brings the mirror back to Merlin will the wizard give him the bell. To get the great book of enchantments requires another quest, this time deep into the gnomish mines. If the hero cannot steal the book, he will have to kill the Ogre Lord to get it, but that means he'll have to find a ring of invisibility and the boots of stealth. . . . Finally, the candelabrum is in the keep of the vampire lord. This means entering the land of the undead. Protection from the undead might be found by wearing a mummy wrapping, but that means digging up a tomb, and that means angering the grave's inhabitant. And of course, there's a dragon somewhere in the neighborhood. If the knight kills it, he can make armor out of its scales; but if he tames it, its fiery breath will defend him against the water demons that are chasing him because he accidentally defiled the sacred fountain by washing his socks in it. Oh, and by the way, the ring of invisibility is cursed and he can't get it off his finger, unless he prays to the god Loki, except Loki is very displeased with him, and that's *really* bad news, so he'd better find a temple and offer the sacrifice of a slain black unicorn—and then Loki will be pleased and maybe remove the curse. But at least, the unicorn horn will cure his acid stomach, so it isn't all bad news.

Notice that the problem just gets more and more complicated. Every part of it is connected to every other part. The good news is that your heroic knight will probably gain a lot of experience and knowledge (and weaponry) along the way, which will give him the confidence and strength and tools he needs to win the amulet from the gray wizard when he finally gets to the castle of Moloch. Of course, then he has to get *out* of the castle, and those air elementals are *really* nasty.

You could write the above story, but it wouldn't be a very good one, because even though all the parts of the problem are connected, there's really no underlying logic. It's just a hodgepodge of fantastic elements all thrown together in one fabulous landscape.

To really make your story work in a way that surprises and delights the reader, all the separate parts of the story should reveal a much larger picture that explains everything.

It's kind of like putting together a jigsaw puzzle. At first, you've got a big collection of colorful pieces. You start by assembling the edges. Then you start filling in toward the center. At the beginning, nothing looks like it fits with anything else, but as you work, you begin to get a sense of what's missing. The more pieces you place, the more you fill the gaps, and the more you realize what you still need to find. Pretty soon, you're looking for a red squiggly piece to fit this hole and a blue jiggly piece to fit into that one. And then suddenly, you plop the last piece in, and you can see the whole picture complete, and you don't really see the separate pieces anymore. Reading a story is like that. *Writing* a story is even *more* like that.

What would make the above example a much better story is if all of the separate parts of the problem were integral. Try this: Suppose the Amulet of Yendor represents such power that it wasn't safe to entrust it to anyone, so King Arthur had the three jewels of power removed and carried to the far ends of the kingdom. The ruby gives the bearer strength, the emerald increases his wisdom, and the bluestone adds to his magical powers. When all three jewels are restored to the amulet, the power of it is integrated. The hero must go out on three separate quests, one for each jewel, in order to restore the amulet to its full power— and each of those separate quests must specifically challenge the hero: first his strength, then his wisdom, finally his understanding of the nature of magic. Each of those challenges should teach him a lesson and confer a tool. Each is preparation—because the bad news is that the wearer of the amulet must confront evil Moloch risen from the grave. But, empowered by his journey, he should integrate not only the jewels into the Amulet of Yendor, but the tools he's been given into a weapon which can defeat Moloch—if only he has the strength, wisdom, and magic to use it.

Afterward, after he defeats Moloch (of course), he must recognize the overwhelming danger that the power of the amulet represents: He will be tempted, like Frodo with the One Ring. Ultimately, he must choose to destroy the amulet, thus demonstrating (again) his strength, wisdom, and magic—and also guaranteeing that this is a once-in-a-lifetime quest. Because that's the way these things are *supposed* to work. That doesn't mean you *have* to do it that way—but your audience has expectations that this is how you *will* do it; so if you choose to break the formula, you have to do it in a way that still resolves the dilemma you set up at the beginning.

In a science fiction story, the details of the "quest" must be even more integrated, because you have to work in the realm of believable science.

For instance, suppose your hero is trying to determine the nature of the alien ecology that's infesting the Earth. He has to see all the separate pieces of it—and the best way to learn is for him to be caught up in the dangers. He climbs down into an alien nest and retrieves eggs and other samples of the alien species. Later, his helicopter is brought down by a "sandstorm" of spores; trapped inside, he observes a whole food-chain of creatures on the windshield. He visits a science center where they have dissected full-grown gastropedes (giant alien worms) and discovered that they have multiple redundant internal organs, so they're almost unkillable. Then he gets captured by renegades, who demonstrate how to "tame" a baby gastropede, and discovers that the aliens have no more natural intelligence than a dog. The mysteries pile up—how can a species with no intelligence mastermind an invasion? Finally, he ends up in the middle of a giant alien settlement where he sees how all the creatures live together, how all of their reproductive strategies are interwoven—and how the whole alien ecology really works. When he returns to civilization, he's infected with all the different parts of the alien ecology that can live in a human body; practically an alien himself, he's neither alien nor human but something psychotic in-between. But locked inside his head is the information that human beings need to understand the alien infestation. Now, as the hero struggles back toward rationality, he begins to haltingly report what he knows—that there are no aliens. They're all just symbiotic colonies, cooperatives of lesser beings. Therefore, if the life cycles of the lesser creatures are destroyed, the multiple symbioses will collapse. Or perhaps they'll evolve again? The ecology must be self-correcting. . . . But because our hero has been changed by his experiences, where is his loyalty? Does he still want to destroy the alien ecology? Or does he now know that it can never be defeated? Does he now think that humanity will have to become a part of it to survive? And is that an accurate view—or is it the aftereffects of living with the aliens?

Notice that in both examples, all the separate parts of the problem eventually bring the hero to the critical decision of the entire problem. Not only that, but in both examples, the hero himself is tested.

The hero's discovery of the nature of the problem must put him up against the biggest test of all—the test of the *Self*.

Structure, Structure, Structure!

All writing is list-making. Nothing more. The trick is knowing what to put next on the list.

At the 1995 World Science Fiction Convention, held in Glasgow, Scotland, one of the attractions was two *huge* barrels of Lego bricks. While they were ostensibly part of the "children's program," there were quite a few adults sitting and playing with the bricks too. People like to put things together. People like to exercise their imaginations.

The thing about Lego bricks is that you can build just about anything you can imagine—if you're patient enough. People have built whole cities out of Lego bricks. The problem is that you have to figure it out yourself how to put the things together. While there might be instructions on how to build a specific kind of Lego castle, there are *no* instructions on how you can build the castle that exists in your own imagination. You have to figure that out yourself.

Planning your story is the same experience. You have a sense of what you want it to be, how you want the pieces to fit together, but actually getting this brick to fit next to that one. . . . Pretty soon, you start to wonder how the hell Arthur C. Clarke and Larry Niven and Frederik Pohl and

Richard Matheson and Jack Finney and Anne McCaffrey and C.J. Cherryh and Connie Willis can make it look so easy.

Here's a trick.

Get yourself a stack of index cards. Write a one-line synopsis of each specific scene that you think should be in your story, one scene per card. Don't worry about writing them down in any specific order. Just write them down as fast as you think of them:

- Lt. Uhura brings a tribble aboard the *Enterprise*.
- Lt. Uhura first gets the tribble from a local merchant.
- Uhura's tribble has a litter of little tribbles.
- Scotty discovers tribbles in the air vents.
- Kirk finds a tribble on his captain's chair.
- Kirk and Spock beam over to the space station. Kirk opens up the storage compartments and lots of tribbles fall down on his head.

But this isn't enough for a complete story. You need a second plot line too, something to complicate the first one:

- A Klingon war cruiser arrives at the same space station.
- The Klingons want shore leave, but what they *really* want is . . .

Oops, wait. Gotta have a motivation for the Klingons. Hmmm.

- The Klingons want shore leave, but what they *really* want is . . . to disrupt the plan for Sherman's Planet.
- The Klingons are on the space station. A barroom brawl breaks out.
- Kirk investigates the fight. He bawls out Scotty and restricts him to quarters. Scotty is glad for the chance to read his technical manuals.

- The plan for Sherman's Planet is that Earth will plant a new grain. If nothing earthlike will grow, the Klingons get the planet.
- The Klingons are here to poison the grain.
- The tribbles eat the poisoned grain, reproduce like crazy and fall on Kirk's head, but McCoy discovers that they're dying.

Okay, this works very well to complicate things. But now we need another half-plot. (Novels, TV episodes, and movies usually have two-and-a-half story lines.) We need to complicate the complication:

- A Federation bureaucrat named Nilz Baris wants Kirk to put guards around the grain.
- Kirk and Baris don't get along.
- When the grain is poisoned, Baris blames Kirk.
- Kirk—no, McCoy—discovers that Baris's assistant is really the Klingon spy who poisoned the grain. Baris is embarrassed.

Now, you take all these separate cards and shuffle them together and start laying them out on the kitchen table in the order you think they should go. First organize each plot line in its own thread. Then you can go back and forth between the separate threads, picking up the next appropriate scene from each.

When you have all the cards laid out in order, go through them as if you're reading a comic book or a storyboard and see if they read like a story. Is this a logical and inevitable progression of events? If it isn't, start moving cards around— no, this one needs to go before that one; this scene has to follow that scene, this group goes here, not there. Oops, I need a scene to fill in between this one and that one, I need another scene to foreshadow—grab some cards and add:

- A Priority One distress call summons the *Enterprise* to space station *K-7*.
- The station commander explains to Kirk about the grain, quadro-triticale. It's critical to Earth. This is where Kirk meets Baris and it's hate at first sight.

Keep doing this—adding, cutting, rearranging—until you think you have all the scenes the story needs in an order that works.

What you will discover as you do this is that everything is connected to everything else. As the various pieces of the story start fitting together, they affect each other; so you will have to make continual adjustments as you go:

- A Priority One distress call summons the *Enterprise* to space station *K-7*.
- A Klingon war cruiser arrives at the same space station.
- The station commander explains to Kirk about the grain, quadro-triticale. It's critical to Earth. This is where Kirk meets Baris, and it's hate at first sight.
- The plan for Sherman's Planet is that Earth will plant a new grain. If nothing earthlike will grow, the Klingons get the planet.
- The Klingons demand shore leave rights, but what they *really* want is . . . to disrupt the plan for Sherman's Planet.
- The Klingons are here to poison the grain. (But we don't know that yet.)
- Kirk and Baris don't get along. Baris is a pompous bureaucrat.
- Lt. Uhura first gets the tribble from a local merchant. Hm, where does merchant get tribbles? Merchant gets tribbles from passing trader, a somewhat unscrupulous fellow.

- Lt. Uhura brings a tribble aboard the Enterprise.
- Uhura's tribble has a litter of little tribbles.
- Baris demands that Kirk put guards around the grain.
- McCoy takes a tribble to study. McCoy's tribble has a litter of tribbles, showing they breed fast.
- *Enterprise* crew gets shore leave, goes to bar. See trader—call him Cyrano something. He tries to sell them tribbles, but nobody wants any more because they breed so fast.
- Trader tries to sell tribbles to Klingons. Tribbles don't like Klingons.
- A barroom brawl breaks out.
- Kirk investigates the fight. He bawls out Scotty and restricts him to quarters. Scotty is glad for the chance to read his technical manuals.
- Kirk finds a tribble on his captain's chair.
- Scotty discovers tribbles in the air vents.
- Kirk and Spock beam over to the space station. Kirk opens up the storage compartments and lots of tribbles fall down on his head.
- The tribbles eat the poisoned grain, reproduce like crazy and fall on Kirk's head, but McCoy discovers that they're dying.
- Kirk investigates who poisoned the grain. It wasn't Cyrano Jones.
- The Klingons demand an apology for the barroom brawl.
- When the grain is poisoned, Baris blames Kirk.
- Kirk discovers that Baris's assistant is really the Klingon spy who poisoned the grain. (Tribbles don't like Klingons.) Baris is embarrassed.
- Cyrano Jones has to pick up all the tribbles from the bar.
- Scotty beams the tribbles over to the Klingons.

This isn't quite the final order of scenes. It's getting there, but there's still a lot of work to be done—cutting and pasting and tweaking—but this should give you an idea of how the process works. (The rest is left as an exercise for the student.)

Some people like to do their outlining on a computer, but the actual physical act of writing scene synopses down on cards and shuffling them around on the kitchen table is still one of the *best* ways to get a sense of the rhythms of story structure, because it allows you to treat scenes as *units*.

A story is a set of motivational units, strung like pearls on a string. Every scene must serve a specific purpose. Every scene should propel the story forward. *Every scene must make the next scene inevitable.* If a scene doesn't move the characters closer to the resolution of the problem, it will feel like a stoplight on the freeway—cut it and the story will leap forward again. (The rule of thumb is that it doesn't matter how good you think the scene is, or how much you love it—if it doesn't move, it doesn't move. Cut it.)

Some novels are built on long internal dialogues of ideas—*Zen and the Art of Motorcycle Maintenance* is an excellent example of a novel in which moving the story forward is less important than exercising a complex personality through a series of philosophical conundrums and explorations; but most science fiction and fantasy stories are more immediate in their circumstances and require that the hero have a lot more hands-on interaction with people and events.

Generally, you will find that a story line must move through a specific set of beats:

- The stage is set.
- The hero is introduced.
- The situation is introduced and the hero discovers he has a problem.

- The hero attempts action and fails. He is beaten up by the problem.
- The hero gains an understanding of the *nature* of the problem.[11]
- The hero takes direct and knowledgeable action.
- The hero discovers everything else that doesn't work. He exhausts all the possibilities he knows. All that is left is what he doesn't know.
- Some event occurs or some person says something that *triggers* the hero's realization of what he needs to do.
- The hero has a personal and self-generated transformation—a shift in being, a reinvention of self—and confronts the problem directly.
- Out of the confrontation, the problem is resolved. The hero is changed by his journey.

The most important of all these beats is the *transformation*. Once you understand the transformation that your hero is headed toward, everything else falls into place as the necessary setup. It's like telling a joke—the transformation is the punch line—so you have to set it up with an enormous amount of anticipation and a lot of surprise in the delivery.

---

[11] I call this scene the *flipover*. It's the scene in which the hero gains a critical understanding of the nature of the situation; after this scene, the mood of the story shifts significantly, because now the hero has a different sense of urgency and direction.

Transformation

Every problem you've ever had in your life—
they all had one thing in common:
You were there.

The transformation of the character is the reason you're telling the story.

A story is an account of how a person who started out like *that* ends up like *this*. How did Luke Skywalker, the teenager, become Luke Skywalker, the Jedi Knight? That's why a story is about the single most important event in the hero's life. (And if it isn't, then *why* are you telling *this* story?)

Transformation occurs when every other alternative has been exhausted. Transformation occurs because there is no other possibility. Transformation occurs because the self is exhausted—it surrenders to the moment. And then surprises itself—by reinventing itself.

Transformation is the reinvention of the self by the Self. The possibility of transformation exists inside every problem. Transformation is a natural skill of human beings. It is startling, astonishing, and miraculous.

The process is so simple it's embarrassing.

Remember what causes a problem to occur? The hero looks at the situation and says, "I can't handle this." By that singular act of resistance, the hero guarantees that the situation will not only persist but get worse. Most problems aren't about handling the problem. They're about *not* handling the problem.

By choosing to make this situation the problem, the hero creates *himself* as the *source* of the problem. Until he recognizes his own authorship of the dilemma, he cannot create himself as *the source* of the resolution.

The *only* possible resolution for the hero is to destroy his relationship of resistance to the problem and replace it with one of ownership. Ownership requires responsibility, and that means that the hero must give up whatever investment he has in not solving the problem and grow the teeth to chew what he has already bitten off. He must step outside the paradigm of little-*self* and invent a larger paradigm of big-*Self*.

The moment of transformation begins when the hero recognizes: *"I'm the problem!"*

And that usually requires that someone or something *first* give the hero a good swift kick in the ass. The hero has to be *awakened to the possibility* that there is *another* way to think about this, another way to *be*.[12]

Transformation requires that the hero see the possibility of it—and the reader as well. The story requires this "trigger moment" so the audience can participate in and understand this most important moment of the character's journey.

The moment in which the hero recognizes, "I'm the problem—" he also recognizes the corollary: *"—therefore I'm the solution!"* His commitment becomes "I *can* handle this. I *will* handle this."

So transformation is not only the re-creation of the hero as the owner of the situation, it is *self-empowerment* as well.

Transformation is always an extraordinary event; it does not occur in the ordinary process of life, it occurs as a break

---

[12] "Luke, use the Force!"

in the ordinary process. In mainstream literature, the transformation of the hero is a personal event; it resolves a specific practical dilemma—but in science fiction, as well as in fantasy, the transformation of the hero is almost always extraordinary to the world as well as to the hero. The character ends up as an elemental force; in effect, he gains superpowers. The transformation is not just metaphorical, it is *real*. Luke becomes a Jedi Knight. Wart becomes King Arthur. Paul Muad'Dib becomes the Kwisatz Haderach. Gully Foyle becomes the man who can jaunt through space *and* time. David Bowman becomes the star child. In the process of transformation, not only is the hero changed, but the world in which he exists is also transformed.

After the hero experiences his or her transformation, the problem is no longer a problem, it's just something to handle. When the problem is handled, it disappears. That usually takes less than ten minutes.

And then the story is over.

Theme

Most writers are also voracious readers. Most writers have favorite authors whose work they seek out. As you become more and more familiar with your favorite author's writing, you will begin to detect an underlying theme—a sense of the author's mind-set and worldview.

For instance, if you read Victor Hugo's *Les Miserables,* you will be struck by the balance he strikes between idealism and cynicism, duty and *higher* duty. The character of Jean Valjean is nicely balanced not only by Javert but by the Thenardiers and Marius as well. Hugo is telling us that life presents challenges, how we accept those challenges determines what kinds of lives we will lead.

If you read the works of Charles Dickens, you will encounter a rare love of language, a skilled insight into the human condition, a powerful streak of irony and outrage, all tempered with an enormous affection for people of good will. Coming into the modern realm, if you read Trevanian, you find that many of his characters represent jaded competence dragged back into action. Tom Clancy's heroes represent idealism and competence, the kind of people we want to be.

In the science fiction domain, the stories of Robert A. Heinlein are almost always about the competent man, or at least how he became *the competent man.* The works of Jack Vance are deliciously nasty and ironic. Harlan Ellison's stories are a scream of consciousness—outrage at the immorality of the universe. Anne McCaffrey's stories are romantic and adventurous, but well cognizant of the discipline necessary for success. Theodore Sturgeon relished the complex dance of emotions when the lives of human beings intersect; he celebrated the joy of being human like no other author in the genre. Spider Robinson is the only living author who comes close to Sturgeon's love of humanity; his stories are about healing and celebration—combining a healthy mix of music, laughter, and dreadful puns. Isaac Asimov's stories are a testimonial to science in all its forms; he celebrated intelligence for its own sake. Roger Zelazny celebrated adventure. A.E. Van Vogt operated in a dream-time of his own making. Alfred Bester was a firework explosion of style, idea, and aspiration toward the stars. J.R.R. Tolkien loved the details of the world he created so much that he painted them with painstaking care. Every author has his own way of looking at life. And every author demonstrates it with every story.

Some authors love their characters and take them on marvelous journeys. Some authors love their ideas and explode them in cascades of extrapolation. Some authors engage in political or sexual screeds. (And sacrifice the story on the altar of ideology—Ayn Rand is the best example.) Some authors are self-indulgent to the point of shamelessness. And some authors demonstrate such a truly admirable engagement with humanity that they justify the invention of language as a tool of communication.

When I have had these discussions with writing classes, the question is invariably asked, "What's your *theme?*"

This is a question that every writer should ponder. "Just why am I writing? What am I saying? What effect am I having on the reader? What effect do I want to produce?"

In my life, I've noticed that situations continue to occur that drag me out of my comfortable chair and put me on the front lines of confrontation and growth. These are called *adventures*. And as a result of every adventure, I've learned something not only about the world but also about myself—I've become a better person for having been thrust headlong into my own life.

So when folks ask me what's my theme, I say, "I'm *the involuntary human.*" I'm the guy who was blithely and unconsciously heading along his own comfortable rut, until life dragged me, kicking and screaming every inch of the way, into my own humanity. And my stories reflect that. My stories are about people waking up to the adventures of their own lives.

What are *your* stories about?

Style

The way you say it is not more important than what you have to say—it just feels that way.

The third-best writing instructor I ever had wasn't a writing instructor at all. He was an art teacher. (I was an art major for two years. I got just good enough to recognize how bad I was.)

Every week, we would study the style of a different artist. Georges Seurat painted in little dots like the phosphors on a color TV screen; Henry Moore saw things as round bulbous shapes with holes in them; Pablo Picasso (in his cubist period) sliced the world into planes that folded and overlapped; and Georges Roualt outlined figures and objects with thick black lines. Our assignment was to create our own drawings or paintings in the style of the artist we had just studied.

It was a liberating exercise. Over the course of the semester, the class tried on a dozen different styles. We peeked at life through different eyes every week, and we discovered that no specific way was the *only* way or the *right* way. We learned that there were many ways to look at things, depending on the effect we wanted to create.

I now regard that art class as one of the most enlightening classes I ever took in college. At some point, early in my career, I began to apply the same idea to storytelling: What challenge can I set myself this time out?

What can I learn from writing in first person instead of third? Is it possible to write a story in second person? Which works best for me, past tense or present? How do I write a love scene?

More important, how can I achieve some of the effects of the *masters* in the field? How can I evoke a magical world like Samuel R. Delaney or Jack Vance? How can I create a feeling of been-there believability like Robert A. Heinlein or Arthur C. Clarke? How can I make the language dance like Alfred Bester or Harlan Ellison?

The more I wrote, the more these questions grew in importance to me. I didn't just want to write, I wanted to write *well*—I wanted to *grow*. That meant I had to move beyond what I knew and take on new challenges each time out. That became a commitment—each and every project would represent a specific challenge. Each and every project must provide the opportunity to learn a new skill or expand an existing one.

Over the next few decades, I continued that commitment. Not every challenge succeeded as I intended, but I learned something new about writing from every attempt—and in that regard, I did succeed. I wrote *Starhunt* in present tense, *Moonstar Odyssey* in metric prose, *Under the Eye of God* and *A Covenant of Justice* in E-Prime. (A linguistic discipline that eschews, the use of the existential verb *to be*. An in-depth discussion of E-Prime can be found in the chapter entitled "To Be or Naught to Be.") And *Jumping off the Planet* I wrote as an evocation of a Heinlein juvenile.

Not every writer wants to make this kind of commitment. Not every writer should. You need to find your own voice, one that works for you. Exploring the tools that work for other writers gives you the chance to look through their eyes, but if the tools don't work for you, don't use them.

Think of style as clothing for your story. Wear the clothes that work for the moment. If you're going to wrestle on the front lawn with the Labrador retriever, you wear ratty old blue jeans and a torn T-shirt. If you're going to the movies, you wear something casual and comfortable, khakis and a sweatshirt. If you're going to a job interview, you wear a suit and tie. If you're going to your wedding, you wear a tuxedo. If you're going to a nude mud-wrestling event . . .

Your writing style, whatever you choose, whatever you create, whatever you evoke, will determine what effects you can create. Style becomes the flavor of the story; you want it to represent the quality of the world you are inviting the reader into. If the moment is romantic, the language should be passionate; if the moment is heavy on technical details, the language should be methodical; if the moment is descriptive, the language should be evocative.

But most of all, the language should always be clear. Short simple sentences convey meaning. Short simple sentences convey meaning much more effectively than overly long, heavily detailed, baroque confections of linguistic fantasy, which, while they may demonstrate the elegance and grace of an author's stylistic trajectories, ultimately, somewhere between apogee and splashdown, the reader's ability to assimilate the conceptualization will become so unfocused that the eventual effect of the sentence is not to edify, but anesthetize.

In other words, you might think your sentence brilliant, but do have mercy on the poor reader who has to decode it. *Eschew obfuscation!*

First Lines

The most important line in your story is the last line—but the reader is never going to get there, unless you have a first line that makes him want to keep reading.

Here are some first lines that work very well. See how many you can recognize.

1. No one would have believed in the last years of the nineteenth century that this world was being watched keenly and closely by intelligences greater than man's and yet as mortal as his own; that as men busied themselves about their various concerns they were scrutinized and studied, perhaps almost as narrowly as a man with a microscope might scrutinize the transient creatures that swarm and multiply in a drop of water.

2. *3 May, Bistritz.*—Left Munich at 8:35 P.M., on 1st May, arriving at Vienna early next morning; should have arrived at 6:46, but train was an hour late.

3. It was a bright cold day in April, and the clocks were striking thirteen.

4. As Gregor Samsa awoke one morning from uneasy dreams he found himself transformed in his bed into a gigantic insect.

5. Once upon a time there was a Martian named Valentine Michael Smith.

6. A squat grey building of only thirty-four stories.

7. Mr. Jones, of the Manor Farm, had locked the henhouses for the night, but was too drunk to remember to shut the popholes.

8. She was a girlygirl and they were true men, the lords of creation, but she pitted her wits against them and she won.

9. *"Charlie Johns,"* urgently cried Charlie Johns: "Charlie Johns, Charlie Johns!" for that was the absolute necessity—to know who Charlie Johns was, not to let go of that for a second, for anything, ever.

10. I'll make my report as if I told a story, for I was taught as a child on my homeworld that Truth is a matter of the imagination.

11. In the box was a belt.

12. To be the skipper of the only boat on the Moon was a distinction that Pat Harris enjoyed.

13. This was a Golden Age, a time of high adventure, rich living, and hard dying ... but nobody thought so.

14. The island of Gont, a single mountain that lifts its

peak a mile above the storm-racked Northeast Sea, is a land famous for wizards.

15. I always get the shakes before a drop.

16. One summer afternoon Mrs. Oedipa Maas came home from a Tupperware party whose hostess had put perhaps too much kirsch in the fondue to find that she, Oedipa, had been named executor, or she supposed executrix, of the estate of one Pierce Inverarity, a California real estate mogul who had once lost two million dollars in his spare time but still had assets numerous and tangled enough to make the job of sorting it all out more than honorary.

Did you recognize these stories?

1. *The War of the Worlds*, by H.G. Wells
2. *Dracula*, by Bram Stoker
3. *1984*, by George Orwell
4. *Metamorphosis*, by Franz Kafka
5. *Stranger in a Strange Land*, by Robert A. Heinlein
6. *Brave New World*, by Aldous Huxley
7. *Animal Farm*, by George Orwell
8. *The Ballad of Lost C'mell*, by Cordwainer Smith
9. *Venus Plus X*, by Theodore Sturgeon
10. *The Left Hand of Darkness*, by Ursula K. LeGuin
11. *The Man Who Folded Himself*, by David Gerrold
12. *A Fall of Moondust*, by Arthur C. Clarke
13. *The Stars My Destination*, by Alfred Bester
14. *A Wizard of Earthsea*, by Ursula K. LeGuin
15. *Starship Troopers*, by Robert A. Heinlein
16. *The Crying of Lot 49*, by Thomas Pynchon

Notice that these first lines either set the stage or hook you into the character. (And those that hook you immediately into the hero's dilemma almost always follow the hook with a bit of stage setting.)

The first line of the story should be just surprising enough to tease you into reading the second line and the third and all the rest. Let your first line have a bit of mystery to it, and the reader will keep going so he can understand why you said what you did.

Pablo Picasso (you may have heard of him, he painted) once said, "All art is recovery from the first line." Although he was talking about drawing and painting, it applies equally well to storytelling. Once you've written a killer first line, the rest of the story is the recovery.

Here are some first lines that don't have stories yet:

Neil Armstrong stared in horror at the bug spots on the windshield of the Lunar lander. . . .

The kids had left a bottle of eyes in the refrigerator.

What I'm about to tell you happened a long time ago—even before the dragon ate grandpa.

North of the city, far enough north that Saturday night is just a dim glow on the horizon, where the old highway curls off between mustard hills, there's a dirt road turnout, easy to miss; the wooden sign has long since fallen away, and the road doesn't seem like much more than a bulldozed firebreak, but if you follow it up to where the canyon dead-ends abruptly against the high cliffs, you'll find something very interesting.

The alien spacecraft looked like a wedge of cheese.

I wake up, and I don't know who I am; I remember just enough to know that this isn't the first time.

You can get used to the gravity in a week, but you never get used to the smell of the air.

Somewhere over the forty yard line, the football decided it had had enough—it bounced off the fingers of the receiver and kept going, scurrying toward the nearest exit as fast as its stubby little legs could carry it.

Aside from the bad breath problem, being a vampire is a lot of fun; you get to meet a lot of interesting people—and kill them.

It wasn't until *after* I died that anyone bothered to explain.

"I'm not very happy about this," the cocker spaniel said quietly; actually he *mrmfled* it—like most dogs, his diction was lousy; only understandable if you listened carefully.

The Mesozoic was not my first choice.

"Sign here, please," said Satan, pushing the contract across the table.

How many of those hooked you? Which ones left you wanting to know what was going to happen next? Or what had already happened? Which ones made you want to know *who* was involved?

Notice how most of these opening lines carry the implication of a larger context that needs to be explored. *What* made the bug spots? *Why* is there a bottle of eyes in the refrigerator—and what kind of eyes are they? *What's* in the canyon? *Where* was the football going? *Why* do dogs talk—and *what* was the cocker spaniel unhappy about? If the Mesozoic wasn't a first choice, what was—and *why?* And *what's* in that satanic contract?

Here's an exercise: Write a dozen first lines of your own, and see which ones make you want to write the next paragraph and the next. Then start writing and see what each line demands. What do you have to do to "recover" from that first line? Keep writing until you have written everything you have to say.

It doesn't matter if it makes sense. It doesn't matter if you have a story. It doesn't matter if you don't know where you're going. The point of this exercise is to demonstrate that good first lines demand first pages—and good first pages demand first chapters. If you can write an interesting opening line, it will not only hook the reader into continuing—it will hook the writer too.

This trick is called *spontaneous invention.* Sometimes your spontaneous inventions will grow into very successful stories—and sometimes they won't.[13] This can be a very effective technique for getting that first mental olive out of the bottle. It's one of the most enjoyable of all writing exercises, because it lets you practice creating just for the fun of creating.

---

[13] Someday, I'd like to publish a collection of all my spontaneous inventions—nothing but story fragments in search of a larger reality. It would probably be a very frustrating book. . . .

Last Lines

Getting into a story effectively is the hard part of the job. Getting out even more effectively is the *harder* part.

Here are some effective last lines. See how many you recognize.

1. And strangest of all is it to hold my wife's hand again and to think that I have counted her, and that she has counted me, among the dead.

2. "We want no proofs; we ask none to believe us! This boy will some day know what a brave and gallant woman his mother is. Already he knows her sweetness and loving care; later on he will understand how some men so loved her, that they did dare much for her sake."

3. Two gin-scented tears trickled down the sides of his nose. But it was all right, everything was all right, the struggle was finished. He had won the victory over himself. He loved Big Brother.

4. And it was like a confirmation of their new dreams and excellent intentions that at the end of their journey their daughter sprang to her feet first and stretched her young body.

5. He left, and Mike pushed back his halo and got to work. He could see a lot of changes he wanted to make—

6. Slowly, very slowly, like two unhurried compass needles, the feet turned towards the right; north, north-east, east, south-east, south, south-south-west; then paused, and, after a few seconds, turned as unhurriedly back twards the left. South-south-west, south, south-east, east. . . .

7. The creatures outside looked from pig to man, and from man to pig, and from pig to man again; but already it was impossible to say which was which.

8. Jestocost lay back on his pillow and waited for the day to end.

9. They began to wait.

10. "I should like to hear that tale, my Lord Envoy," said old Esvans, very calm. But the boy, Therem's son, said stammering, "Will you tell us how he died?—Will you tell us about the other worlds out among the stars—the other kinds of men, the other lives?"

11. All right, I accept.
    I am going to put on the belt.

12. Then he walked back to the controls to take *Selene II* on his last voyage, and her maiden one, across the Sea of Thirst.

13. She bathed Foyle gently and then set the tray before him as an offering. Then she settled down alongside Joseph . . . alongside the world . . . prepared to await the awakening.

14. Their hearts were very light as they entered into the firelight and warmth under that roof; and Yarrow ran to meet them, crying with joy.

15. "To the everlasting glory of the Infantry—"

16. The auctioneer cleared his throat. Oedipa settled back, to await the crying of lot 49.

Did you recognize these stories?

1. *The War of the Worlds*, by H.G. Wells
2. *Dracula*, by Bram Stoker
3. *1984*, by George Orwell
4. *Metamorphosis*, by Franz Kafka
5. *Stranger in a Strange Land*, by Robert A. Heinlein
6. *Brave New World*, by Aldous Huxley
7. *Animal Farm*, by George Orwell
8. *The Ballad of Lost C'mell*, by Cordwainer Smith
9. *Venus Plus X*, by Theodore Sturgeon
10. *The Left Hand of Darkness*, by Ursula K. LeGuin
11. *The Man Who Folded Himself*, by David Gerrold
12. *A Fall of Moondust*, by Arthur C. Clarke
13. *The Stars My Destination*, by Alfred Bester
14. *A Wizard of Earthsea*, by Ursula K. LeGuin
15. *Starship Troopers*, by Robert A. Heinlein
16. *The Crying of Lot 49*, by Thomas Pynchon

The last line is the punch line. It is the last great chord

in a grand symphony. It is the last two beats of "shave-and-a-haircut-two-bits." It is "Th-th-that's all, folks!" It is your exit line.

A great last line should leave your reader satisfied that you have said everything that needs to be said—and at the same time, it should stand as a launch pad for the reader's imagination to leap off into its own flight of fantasy about what happens next.

Notice how most of the last lines above carry the implication that the story will continue even after the writer stops reporting? An effective exit should leave you wondering—*speculating*—what will happen next, especially if the last line says or suggests that the hero is waiting. What *will* happen when lot 49 is cried?

Just as the opening line should suggest a larger context that needs to be explored, so should the last line leave the reader with the responsibility to explore it himself in the privacy of his own head.

Some last lines are all-purpose. You can use them anywhere. Which is probably why you shouldn't use them at all.[14]

"There are some things that man was not meant to know."

That's not for us to know. Only history will tell.

"I don't know, but we'll think of something."

"But that's another story for another time—"

"No, it's not the end. It's the *beginning*. . . ."

---

[14] Clichés are a dime a dozen. Avoid them like the dickens.

That was the last time I saw him.

"Take us home—"

And then she woke up—

"There's no place like home!"

Here's an exercise: Write a dozen last lines of your own—and see which ones make you want to tell the story that precede them.

She dropped the blood-stained knife on the table. "Next time, do your own dirty work."

Punch Lines

*Meet me halfway! The cow and the
penguin don't drink tea!*

Think of your story as a joke. It has three parts. The first
part sets up the situation. The second part demonstrates
the nature of it. The third part resolves it in a satisfying
way, usually outrageous.

Here are some jokes:

The Beginning: Mr. Goldberg goes up to the roof and
starts calling, "Hey, God! This is Goldberg talking.
You know me. I'm a good man. Talk to me, God!" He
does this for a long while, until finally God answers.
"WHAT IS IT, GOLDBERG?"

"Listen God, I've never asked for anything. I've
always given, so I thought, maybe just once if I asked,
you could grant my wish."

"WHAT IS IT, GOLDBERG?"

"I would like to win the New York State Lotto, so
I could do good things for other people."

God thinks about it and says: "CONSIDER IT
DONE."

The Middle: A week later, Goldberg goes up on the
roof again and starts calling, "Hey, God. It's been a
week already. You promised me I would win the New
York State Lotto, but so far, I haven't won. Listen,
how hard could that be? You created the Earth in six
days, so a little thing like the Lotto, I mean, all right,

already, okay? I'm a patient man, God, but you know I'm old, and I'd like to have some time to do some good. I just want you to know I'm still here and I'm still waiting and I expect you to keep your promise."

The End: Another week goes by. Goldberg returns to the roof. "So, listen, God, you made a promise, two weeks have gone by and nothing has happened. Is this any way for the ruler of the universe to behave? I mean, if I can't trust God, who can I trust—?"

Suddenly, there is a clap of thunder and God responds: "GOLDBERG. MEET ME HALFWAY. BUY A TICKET."

The Beginning: A Hindu, a Jew, and a lawyer (yes, this is one of those stories) are driving along one night when their car breaks down. They hike to the only farmhouse in the neighborhood. The farmer says, "It's too late for a truck to come out tonight. You can sleep here, but I only have two beds. One of you will have to sleep in the barn."

They draw straws and the Jew loses. He goes out to sleep in the barn.

A few moments later, there is a knock on the door. The farmer answers. The Jew is standing there. He says, "I'm sorry, but there is a pig in that barn. In my religion, pigs are unclean. I cannot sleep in the barn with a pig."

The Middle: The Hindu and the lawyer draw straws and the Hindu loses. He goes out to the barn.

A few moments later, there is a knock on the door. The farmer answers it. The Hindu is standing there. He says, "I'm sorry, but there is a cow in that barn. Cows are sacred to my faith. I cannot sleep in that barn."

The End: The lawyer sighs and says, "All right, I'll go." He goes out to the barn.

A few moments later, there is a knock on the door. The farmer answers it. The cow and the pig are standing there.

The Beginning: Just outside of Dublin, there's a little convent, called Our Lady of Perpetual Indulgence. One evening, Mother Superior Sister Mary Godzilla is sitting and doing the books, paying the bills, when two leprechauns appear on her desk, a big one and a little one. The little one is laughing hysterically and poking the big one. "Go ahead, ask her, ask her."

The big leprechaun hushes the little one and turns to the Mother Superior and politely asks for a moment of her time. "How many leprechaun nuns have you got in this convent?"

The Mother Superior says, "I'm sorry to disappoint you, but we have no leprechaun nuns in this convent." This news makes the little leprechaun laugh so hard he falls down, shouting, "I told ye, I told ye."

The Middle: The big leprechaun smacks the little one upside the head and says to the Mother Superior, "Can I ask you another question then? How many leprechaun nuns are there in all of Ireland?"

The Mother Superior says, "Well, I have done a bit of traveling for the archdiocese, and I must tell you that if there were any leprechaun nuns in Eire, I think I would have heard, and I've never heard of any."

This news makes the little leprechaun laugh so hard, he falls off the desk, shouting, "I told ye, I told ye."

The End: The big leprechaun smacks the little one with his shillelagh, and turns back to the Mother Superior. "Well, then let me ask you, how many leprechaun nuns are there in the whole of Christendom, in all of the church?"

The Mother Superior says, "Look, I've tried to be polite. I didn't want to hurt your feelings. But there aren't any leprechaun nuns anywhere."

At this, the little leprechaun wets his shorts laughing. "I told ye, I told ye. Ye focked a penguin!"

The Beginning: A man is driving along through the Australian outback when his car breaks down. He hikes for miles until he comes to a set of three dilapidated shacks. One of them has a sign that says, "CAFÉ." He goes in and sits down at the counter and says, "Water. Bring me water, please."

The café owner says, "That would be suicide. The water here is so bad, you wouldn't even flush a toilet with it."

The Middle: "All right, then," says the traveler. "Beer. Bring me beer."

The café owner says, "I'm sorry, but this is the town of Mercy. We are a religious community. We don't serve alcohol."

The traveler says, "Well, then bring me a Coke."

But the café owner says, "I'm sorry, but we don't serve soft drinks here. We're so far from anywhere else that we can't afford to have them shipped in."

The End: The traveler is mystified. "You can't drink the water, you don't serve alcohol, and there are no soft drinks. What do you drink here?"

The café owner says, "We brew a special tea in the

pouch of the koala bear. It makes the water palatable."

"All right, I'll have that."

The café owner brings him two big mugs of hot steaming tea. He eagerly drinks. Almost immediately, he spits it out. "Yichh. This tea is full of hair!!"

"Fur. That's the fur of the koala bear."

"Why didn't you strain it out?!!"

The owner looks offended. *"Sir! The koala tea of Mercy is not strained!"*

Notice that in each of these jokes, there is a built-in rhythm of storytelling:

The beginning gives you the situation. The middle gives you a repetition so you'll know exactly what part of the situation is being developed. The end gives you the resolution.

Notice that the last line of the joke is the punch line. Notice that the last word of the punch line is the punch *word:* Buy a *ticket!* The cow and the pig are standing *there!* Ye focked a *penguin!* The koala tea of Mercy is not *strained!*

Let's look at one of my favorite quotes from that great star of stage, screen, and television, Miss Piggy:

"Never eat anything—"

So far, we know that this sentence is unfinished. We know that there's a modifying clause to follow:

"—larger than—"

Ahh, this is going to be a piece of good advice. We are already anticipating eagerly the rest of the news:

"—your head."

Notice, the punch *word* came last. In the beat of silence that follows, you have the opportunity to gasp in surprise. Consider that an even more outrageous punch word makes the line even funnier.

"—a Volkswagen."

Punch words exist even in situations that aren't funny. Remember when Count Dracula says:

"I never drink . . . *wine.*"

Punch words make dialogue work.

The alien ambassador clacked its mandibles politely. "We do not eat our prey live—except, of course, on holidays."

Punch words give punch lines impact. Punch lines provide critical closure to dialogue.

An effective punch line makes the point clearly and dramatically. It produces an impact with an economy of language. It has a solid rhythm and it ends on the beat, so there is nothing left to stumble over.

How funny would those jokes have been if the punch lines had been written this way:

Finally, after a long silence, God says, "GOLDBERG. GIVE ME A BREAK. YOU TALK TOO MUCH. AND YOU'RE STUPID. YOU HAVE TO BUY A TICKET IF YOU WANT TO WIN THE LOTTO."

A few moments later, somebody is banging and kicking angrily at the door. The farmer sighs and gets out of bed and goes to answer it. The cow and the pig are standing there. The cow says, "We don't sleep with lawyers, they're unclean and disgusting."

At this, the little leprechaun is beside himself with laughter. He jumps up and down. He waggles his fingers in his ears and sticks out his tongue. He makes lewd and lascivious and obscene gestures. "A penguin, a penguin! You did it with a foul-smelling waterbird, you great galumphing lout! I told ye, but did ye listen to me? No, ye didn't. Ye did it with a penguin, ye stupid git!"

The owner looks offended. *"Sir! You know the old saying about the quality of Mercy. Well, that's our religious commitment. That we don't strain our tea."*

Duh. . . .

Can you see the difference?

It's the difference between making your point effectively and just throwing some words at the page.

The same principles apply to all forms of storytelling, whether you're telling a joke, a love story, a suspense thriller, a fantasy, or a science fiction tale. First, you set up the problem, then you demonstrate the nature of it to build up the suspense, then you conclude with an *impactful* resolution that produces a gasp of outrage, shock, horror, surprise, or delight. *Buy a ticket! The cow and the pig are standing there. Ye focked a penguin. The koala tea of Mercy is not strained.*

The payoff is not only the hero's moment of transformation—it is the *reader's* as well.

Write From Inside

*Satisfy yourself first. That way you know
at least one person had a good time.
(This is only true for storytelling; it is
exactly the opposite for sex.)*

In 1942, Robert A. Heinlein published a serial in *Astounding Science Fiction* called *Beyond This Horizon*. The story takes place a century or two in the future. There's a moment when the hero arrives at a door. Heinlein did *not* describe it this way:

> All the separate panels of the auto-door slid backward into the wall, creating the illusion of an enlarging elliptical opening, like the iris behind a camera lens.

Instead, Heinlein wrote:

> The door dilated.

Nothing else.
Why?
Because nothing more was needed. The door *dilated*. The writer doesn't have to explain how it works. He doesn't have to invent a technology for it. You don't explain doors. You walk through them.

Actually, the full text of Heinlein's paragraph is:

He punched the door with a code combination, and awaited face check. It came promptly; the door dilated, and a voice inside said, "Come in, Felix."

Heinlein's predictions were good. Door code locks are already on the market; the technology for retinal scans and face checks has already been demonstrated. Automatic sliding doors are installed at many supermarkets. These things are taken for granted because we live with them every day—and Heinlein recognized that as part of the human condition too. We only marvel at this stuff *the first time*. After that, it's just scenery.

Suppose you're writing a story that takes place in your own home. The hero goes to leave the room. Do you write:

The door was a wooden panel that filled the door frame. It was mounted on brass hinges, allowing it to swing outward. A round metal handle was mounted waist high on the right side. Joe grabbed the *knob* and twisted it to free the latching mechanism that held the door in place. He pulled, and the door swung open easily. He stepped through, grabbed the *knob* on the other side, and pulled it shut after him. The latch caught automatically. He turned in horror— had he locked himself out?

Or do you write:

He shut the door quietly behind himself and sighed. Yes, this was much easier.

Part of this relies on the reader's own experience with doors, but more importantly, a storyteller has to write his stories as if he has lived them—*you have to write from inside the experience.* This may be the most important of all writing skills.

Just about anyone can describe a T. Rex or a telepathic dragon or a feral Chtorran.[15] But describing is not the same as *evoking.*

Your intention is to have the reader *experience* the story. That means you have to write each moment as if you lived it yourself. You're reporting what it felt like, what it tasted like, what it smelled like. You've been there and have come back to tell about it.

Think about your daily routine. Have you stopped at an ATM recently to get some cash? If you had been writing science fiction in 1950, you might have predicted a bank machine. Would you have had to explain it? Undoubtedly. You might have produced this:

> Mary slid a magnetic card into the machine. She punched a code in the keyboard. The screen cleared and asked her what she wanted. She typed in: WITH-DRAW TWENTY DOLLARS. The machine clunked softly to itself while it telephoned her bank and electronically signaled the transaction. Satisfied with the response, it chimed its approval. After a moment, two bright blue twenty dollar bills rolled out of the machine's printer. She liked the new bills better. Ike's smiling face made the money seem friendlier.
>
> She took a radio-telephone out of her purse and dialed up the ThreeDee theater. "Yes," she said to the woman who answered. "What time is the next showing of *A Martian Romance?*"

Not only is every piece of technology *explained* in this

---

[15] Well, maybe not a feral Chtorran. . . .

circa-1950 paragraph, but there are several misassumptions too. The writer has put in too many details, practically guaranteeing that the story will look quaint and obsolete in only a few years.

Here's how you might write the same paragraph today:

> Still talking on the phone, Mary pulled up to the ATM. Preoccupied, she fumbled her card into the slot and punched for two hundred dollars. She hastily gathered the cash, the receipt, the card, shoved them all into her purse, and honked her way back into traffic; she hadn't missed a beat in the conversation. "Okay, Joe, Jane, Fred—I'll meet you all at the multiplex."

In 1950, the audience didn't have the direct personal experience of credit cards, computers, bank machines, cell phones, or even conference calls. It wasn't in the common vocabulary of ideas. They wouldn't have known that an ATM is an Automated Teller Machine or even how it works. In 1950, the word "machine" conjured up the image of a drill press or a steam shovel, so saying that she withdrew two hundred dollars from a machine would have been an incomplete image. Indeed, if you had said "automated teller machine" to the average reader in 1950, he might have imagined something out of *The Jetsons:* a chrome-plated robotic head and torso with a cash drawer in the belly. (*And* a withdrawal of two hundred dollars would have been extravagant. In 1950, she would have withdrawn only ten or twenty dollars at most. Fifty years of inflation have raised prices by an order of magnitude.)

Fortunately for science fiction writers, most readers today have an extensive science fiction vocabulary. You don't have to explain FTL[16] starships or cellular phones. Even though no one has invented the technology for faster-than-light travel yet, the audience still has the concept—they got it from *Star Trek* and *Star Wars*. The audience also knows droids, cryo-sleep, cyborgs, aliens, biowar, telepathy, sex changes, multiple personalities, psychological reprogramming, nanotechnology, computer viruses, orbital beanstalks, solar sails, genetic engineering, sentient intelligence engines, transporters, and even the basic principles of alien ecology. You might have to demonstrate the details, but it's unlikely that you'll need to stop the story for a science lesson to explain the basic concept. A sentence or two should be sufficient to let them know that *you* understand what you are writing about.

Your readers are likely to have computers and access to the Internet; you have to expect that your audience already has considerable knowledge and expertise. Today's audiences have a different relationship with machinery. They are used to the idea that machines can do just about anything. And most machines today look like boxes with buttons and a screen—so a storyteller only needs to call the machine by a descriptive name and have it produce the result as needed:

> John pushed his hair back and closed his eyes. He leaned forward into the Makeup-Matic and said, "Casual office, day. Fluorescent lighting. I'm wearing the brown suit. Healthy, but not aggressive." A soft tickle of air played across his eyebrows, eyelids, and cheeks. He inspected himself in the mirror—not perfect, but it would have to do, he was in a hurry.

---

[16] FTL is an acronym for faster-than-light, but you probably already knew that.

If you were writing for an audience that was familiar with the concept of automatic makeup machines—if they had such machines in their own bathrooms—you could write:

> John took a minute to do his makeup, and then he was out the door.

By the way, did you notice the *other* cultural assumption those paragraphs challenged? If this is a world where men wear makeup to look good in public, then John is living in a culture that places much more importance on style and manners, and that should be reflected elsewhere in the story too. If John is rushing out to fight alien slugs from the planet Zorg, he's not going to stop to check his eyebrows; but if he's having a meeting with the ambassador from Mars, he most certainly will check his appearance. (And the brown suit would be inappropriate anyway; black would be better. Brown is the Martian color for bereavement after a thirst.)

You don't have to present *all* the information, but you do have to present enough for the reader to understand what's happening—little nuggets of information that wake up the imagination while keeping one foot in reality.

Also remember that you are writing about people who are (usually) familiar with the world they live in. You may intend the scenery to be marvelous and surprising to the reader, but to the characters in the story, it's *ordinary*. They're not going to marvel over it. They take it for granted that this is the way things work. (Does a New Yorker stop to stare up at the Empire State Building in awe every time he passes it? Of course not. Only when a twenty-five-foot gorilla is swatting biplanes out of the air.)

The *real* marvel is that the people in the story take all your marvelous inventions for granted.

The *Star Trek* Mistake (Part Two). Ever notice, on any of *Star Trek*'s various iterations, that whenever these people encounter something, it's always the *first* time anyone has ever encountered it?

They never arrive at a situation with the benefit of prior knowledge. They are always starting from square one. After a while, you start to wonder what kind of an organization Starfleet is, that everything is a surprise to its officers. Fortunately, the people in *Star Trek* are so wonderful, that they always solve the problem just in time for the last commercial.

OK, yes—sometimes your hero is visiting a new world—in that case, a sense of awe is not only appropriate, it's *mandatory*. Lessa is fascinated by the Weyr and the way that humans live in partnership with telepathic dragons (*Dragonflight* by Anne McCaffrey). The crew that discovers Rama are humbled and stunned by this huge interstellar vessel (*Rendezvous With Rama* by Arthur C. Clarke). On an even larger scale, Louis Wu is awestruck by the size of the Ringworld, how it works, and the species that live there (*Ringworld* by Larry Niven).

How the characters in the story react to what is happening around them gives the audience strong emotional cues—they will share the surprise and the wonder, or the horror and the fear. But if the characters in the story do not express surprise, then they are demonstrating that the events they are experiencing are *commonplace* in their lives.

"The gray thing is Ambassador Slith," the aide whispered. "He's very insistent about resolving the transport license problem tonight. He's planning to fission tomorrow."

"I hate it when my brother changes sex without telling me," Martha said. "She's always borrowing my clothes."

"Do you like purple steak?" Mom had *that* tone in her voice. "Because if you don't get this replicator fixed, you'd better get used to it."

"But I was going into Tosche Station to pick up some power converters," Luke protested.

Uncle Owen wasn't fooled. "You can waste time with your friends when your chores are done."

The refrigerator was displaying a new commercial— an overhead shot of fresh Martian anchovies dancing around a pizza. I thought about painting it over once and for all, but first I wanted some juice.

"That'll be four chocolate dollars," said the clerk. "We don't take credit dollars anymore."

"Dragon eggs make wonderful omelettes," said the witch. "But it's hard to get them fresh, and if you don't get them fresh, sometimes the omelette gets you."

There's another point to make here. Even though the situations in these examples are all unusual, notice that each one also has a link back to the reader's own experiences. This is *borrowing credibility*. The reader knows what an annoyed mom sounds like, or why he can't go hang out with friends until his chores are done, or sisters who complain about people going through their things.

All of these subtly draw upon the reader's experiences of how things work in the real world. In these moments, the sense of wonder comes from the collision of real and imaginary, with the imaginary providing the "marvel," while the real provides the ground of believability.

Here's another example: Suppose your hero is on an alien world; he wanders into the local cantina and meets a twelve-meter-long slug from the slime world, Maizlish. You could write:

> The thing was big and it smelled awful—the smell was indescribably rank. Commander Jaxin nearly retched.

That might serve your story, but it won't evoke the experience. The reader won't be convinced that you've been there.

So close your eyes and imagine the experience for yourself. What would it be like to be in a room with a creature the size of a bus? If the thing is from a slime world, it's probably slimy too. Imagine all that slime oozing out of the creature's body, dripping on the floor. What do you think stale slime smells like? What do you think it would be like to touch such an animal? Is there anybody else present? What are they doing? What other questions could you ask?

> Jaxin had seen pictures, but no picture could have prepared him for the incredible smell of the thing— it was like a dirty diaper turned inside out. It was every bad smell he'd ever encountered all rolled up into one—festering sauerkraut, gangrene, sour milk,

vomit, and boiled cabbage. Even through the aggressive filtering of the rebreather, the smell was enough to make him retch.

The creature wasn't exactly shapeless, but it sagged across the floor as if it was aspiring to shapelessness. It was crooning one of its native songs, and its gelatinous flesh rippled in oily waves. Even worse, the slug was *oozing* green mucus of varying consistencies; some of it had dried and hardened, the rest dripped like ichor—the beast looked like a giant singing booger.

Jaxin wondered why the owner allowed slugs in the tavern. They couldn't possibly be good for business. And they'd never get rid of the smell after it left. But none of the other patrons in the bar were paying any attention. It was just a normal Saturday night.

Abruptly, the beast stopped. It swung one end around—the end with all the eyes and a slobbering hole that could have been a mouth. "Hi, sailor," it whistled melodiously. "New in town? Looking for a good time?"

Jaxin shuddered. "Uh, no thanks. I'm an eclectic in a process. And, um—I never have sex outside my own ecology."

Imagine yourself in the scene. See what there is to be seen. Listen to the sounds. Touch the world. Smell the air. Taste it. Use all of your senses.

Then *evoke* those experiences for the reader. If you give the audience the flavor, they'll flesh out the moment in their own imaginations.

Sex Scenes

Sex is friction. Preferably friction with a friend.
After that it's all a matter of taste.

Sex scenes are embarrassing.

They're embarrassing to write. They're embarrassing to read. And most of all, they're embarrassing to publish.

Probably, this is because people will assume you were writing from experience. And if you weren't writing from experience, then why were you writing about *that?* Obviously, you must have been interested in it to write it.

Every time you write a sex scene, you're telling people not just that you think about sex, you're also telling them *what* you think about sex. It is a very public admission of a very private part of your life. And no matter how many times you say, "It's just a story," the fact remains that *you* are the person who sat at the keyboard and imagined it.

People will come up to you for years afterward, and they will mention *that* book or *that* story . . . and you will be certain that they are thinking about *that* scene in that book or that story. You won't be able to help yourself; you'll look to see if their eyes have that extra little sparkle that suggests that just maybe they're interested in finding out if you really are as good as *that* particular scene suggests.

Here's a sex scene I wrote in 1970 for *When Harlie Was One:*

They were in bed and he was poised over her. And still their eyes were locked, an embrace of mutual fascination in which each was reflected in the other's delight. The delight was joyous. And the bed was full of gasps. And sighs. And giggles.

And, oh, there was such an *overflowing* inside of him, such a surge of tension released. All this time, all this time, he had been wanting, wanting, it had been building, gathering like water impatient behind a dam. Somewhere in his past he had known this joy— but somewhere also in his past, he had let it slip away. Now here it was again and it was part of him—the sheer animal delight in the joyous experience of sex and love—all tumbled together and laughing in the sheets.

They paused to rest, to breathe, to share a kiss, to giggle together, to shift slightly, to kiss again. He bent down suddenly and kissed her eyes, first one, then the other.

She looked at him as if seeing him for the first time, and her arms were tight around him. And tighter, her hands were grasping. "Oh, David—"

He held her and he held her and he held her and still he couldn't hold her enough. He was exploding in joy; he could neither contain nor control it. Her little soft gasps were sobs, and he knew why she was crying. He had to wipe at his eyes too.

"Oh—" she said, and kissed him. "Oh, David— I—I—" She kissed him again. "Have you ever seen anyone crying with happiness?"

He wanted to laugh, but he was crying at the same time, sobbing with joy and melting down into her. He was a chip of flesh tossed on a splashing sea of laughter and wet eyes and love. A pink sea, with foamy waves and giggling billows. Rednipple-topped pink seas. "Oh, Annie, Annie, I can't let go of you, I can't—"

"I don't want you to. I don't want you to. Oh, never let go. Never."

"Never . . . never . . . " he gasped. He was moving again now, onto and into her. A joyous thrusting— steel and velvet, flesh and silk, shaft and lining. He was sobbing as he did, sobbing with joy—and she was too.

All the days of wanting and holding back, all those denials of the body and the animal within, all of it poured forth now, incredibly intense—*he could die now, he was complete!*—all melted into flowing tears and eyes shining, sparkling in rapture. It was the sharing! So bright he couldn't stand it! And she was the one he wanted to share it with!

She moved with him, with love and happy giggling lust, the two blending into a whirlpool of sloppy silly kisses. And then once more the waves gathered them up, surging and crashing and gasping, sweeping them high across a sweet sky of delight and at last leaving them gently on the shores of a sighing embrace. The waters lapped at the shore and gentled their touch, and their fingers strayed across the velvety landscape, exploring—familiar and yet always wondrous.

He was holding her tightly. He couldn't stop holding her. She sighed—a sound of pleasure. He echoed it and smiled. Tears were streaming down his cheeks. He laughed. And kissed her. And kissed her.

And kissed her.

They spent Saturday falling in love.

Deeper in love.

It began before either was fully awake, with an

unconscious fitting of their bodies, one to the other, with the purely animal reflex of erection, sliding forward, and he was onto and into her almost as reflex, so familiar was the desire. She eased onto her back, only slowly coming awake. He was aware now; he was inside her, warm and exciting, a silken motion.

She opened her eyes and looked at him. He paused in his motion. "I had the strangest dream," she said. "I dreamed I was being—"

"Shh," he said. "Don't wake me up—I'm still dreaming." And pressed deeper. She brought her legs up to help him.

This time, instead of melting into the experience, he was totally conscious of himself and his body. It was a new awareness he possessed, an awareness of the sexuality inherent in himself and in her. His hands gripped her legs and he pumped at her vigorously, penetrating so deeply he marveled at the sensation of pure power the experience produced.

Poised above her in the silent morning, he was once again aware of how truly beautiful she was—more beautiful in the act of love than he had ever seen her before.

She giggled. "This is silly."

"Isn't it though?" he asked, and they both laughed and kissed and hugged again, embracing through the splashing suds of the shower.

They broke apart and she sudsed his chest again. He let his hands slide up and down across her chest— her breasts, her nipples. Her pink flesh glistened with the flowing water and the foam of the soap. Her green eyes glowed at him. Shone.

She played with the hair on his chest, drawing circles in the sparse little patch; it was almost lost in the suds. She let her hands wander downward, straying into a coarser forest of hair, and lower still, she stroked the length of his penis with one exquisite fingernail, then drew it lower still, outlining his testes with first one finger and then another and finally her whole curious hand. Shyly, she smiled as she watched what her hand was up to. Her fingers came back up slowly, caressing and exploring. His penis was neither soft nor erect, it was somewhere in between. The skin of it was like velvet, and the cap of the glans was tender and pink. Her fingers traced the ridge around the edge of it, and she cupped it in her palm and looked up at him, and they were both smiling and giggling like children in a schoolyard. "Can I touch it?" she asked impishly.

He grinned. "If I can touch yours . . ."

She giggled with a bright squeak as his hands slid down from her breasts. It was as if he had never done this before, never explored the body of a woman before. The names—*mons, pubis, labia majora, labia minora*—all meant nothing before the mystery that was Annie. His finger touched her soft hair, probed the gentle swelling, slipped gently into the opening in her flesh. She was like silk and the splashing of the shower around them was as the spray of the sea.

"You feel so . . . good. . . ." he murmured.

"Mmmmm," she said. "Mmmm hmmmm. If you think it feels good from there, you ought to try it from my side. . . ."

He laughed. She laughed. They had been laughing all morning—even at things that weren't funny. Yet everything was funny today. It was the laughter of delight—of rapturously lovely delight. "Okay," he said. "Change places with me."

Again they laughed. But neither moved their hands from the other's gentle warmth. They stepped a little closer. "Oh, look," she said. "It's growing—and I thought it was all tired out by now."

"Mm," he whispered into her hair. "You keep bringing it up again. . . ."

"Mm hmm, I have just the place for it."

She stepped closer, shifting her stance slightly. "There's no way to do this and still be ladylike," she laughed. She arched herself and began to guide his penis into the space between her legs and up into her self. The firm length of it slipped easily into her—and just as easily out again. "Oops, have to try again."

But he kissed her first, a deep deep penetrating kiss, tongues touching, lips working, soft and gentle and passionate. Their wet and soapy bodies, legs and bellies were pressed together, slippery and exciting. He moved his hand around to her back, to caress her buttocks, then slipped his fingers downward and forward.

She had her hand between the two of them, was holding his penis again. Raising herself up on tiptoes, she slipped it into the depths of her and sighing, eased herself down around and onto and into and she sighed again and he said "Mmmmm."

And then they held each other tightly and pressed hard, moving against each other, moving and moving and keeping it moving in a steady rocking dance, gliding so easily back and forth, stopping only once to readjust themselves so they wouldn't slip, and another time, stopping only for breath and to laugh again.

He lay down on his back in the tub and she lay down on top of him, giggling at the thought. "I've never done it in a bathtub," she admitted, then fit herself around him again, riding him like a steed, moving on him with real excitement now, sliding her body across his, her flesh slipping against his in the gentlest of ecstasies. The warm warm flesh of her breasts slid back and forth across his chest and the steaming water splashed down across her back and down and around the both of them. She lowered her face to his and they kissed again, and after a while he was on top and she was on bottom and the tub was slippery and warm and full of giggles. And sighs. And gasps.

Actually, I cheated. That wasn't *only* a sex scene. It was also a love scene. (About two months after the book was published, a beautiful young woman came breathlessly up to me at a convention and whispered, *"David! I had no idea you were so . . . so passionate."*)

Here's the next part of it:

It was later and they were down.

They were sitting in bed together, eating vanilla ice cream. It was sweet and cold.

And he still loved her.

He looked at her and the tears came unbidden to his eyes, he was so happy. "This is so silly—" he said, wiping at himself.

"No, no—it's all right. Wait. Let me—" She leaned over and kissed his eyes, first one and then the other. She touched his nose with her spoon, leaving a drop of cold whiteness on the tip. Then she leaned forward and licked the ice cream off. "—and guess what I'm going to have for dessert."

"Woman, have you no mercy!" he moaned. "I have a weak heart."

"Can you think of a better way to die?" She looked at him expectantly.

"Uh—no."

"Good. If you have any last wishes, you have fifteen minutes."

He sighed and leaned back against his pillow, the bowl of ice cream forgotten on his lap. He felt so *good*. He wished he could just sit here and *feel* forever.

"This is it," he said. "This is *really* it. It's all about feeling—and I feel so good. . . ."

And suddenly he *knew*.

The thought went *klunk* in his head so loudly, he sat up bolt upright. "My God."

"What? What is it."

"I know. I mean, I know the *answer*."

"To what? To everything?"

"No. Just to HARLIE's question. Love. I know what love is now. I mean, I *know*."

"Well, don't die with it. Tell me."

"Okay—um, wait a minute. Let me say this right. Okay, you ready?"

"David!"

"All right—don't hit. Love is not what you think."

"Huh?"

"Let me say it again. Love is *not* what you *think*."

"How do you know what I think—?"

"It doesn't matter *what* you think. Love is *not* what you *think*. No, no, don't hit! I'll explain. All the talking about love—that's not love. That's talking. All the thinking about love—that's not love either. That's

145

thinking. Love isn't what you say and it isn't what you think. It's what you *feel*. That's all it is. Nothing more. But all that talking and thinking—and all that other stuff we do—that's just stuff that we make up *about* love. It's not love, Annie! We just think it is, because we've made this stupid connection that talking and thinking about something actually have something to do with the thing itself. Love is really very easy. We're the ones who make it so hard."

"I like making it hard," she said innocently. "It works better that way."

"Yes—that's it too!" he said, ignoring her joke and going for the truth behind it. "We put all that stuff in the way to make it seem more worthwhile when we get there. But the truth is, Annie—we're such jerks! Human beings, I mean. It's so easy, it's so natural. I mean . . .—am I babbling? I don't care. I am so fucking happy, it doesn't matter. I'm going to say it all anyway."

He put his ice cream dish down and turned to her, holding her by the shoulders. "And maybe, in some stupid way, this is the answer to everything else too— you know how good we feel right now? Can you imagine anyone hurting another person, *any person at all*, while they felt this good? I can't! All I want to do is spread the feeling around. I want everybody to feel this good. I want to run out into the street and shout, 'Hey, listen up world! It's possible. Love is really possible!' Except they'd lock me up, wouldn't they? They wouldn't believe it. They couldn't dare accept it."

"It'd do wonders for my reputation though," Annie said, smiling gently.

"But you do see it, don't you?"

"Oh, yes. Right now, I cannot imagine why any human being would ever again want to tell a lie or steal or cheat or—I can't imagine murder, let alone war. And yet—" Her eyes went softly sad. "—I know that when we go back *out there* again, all that stuff will come crowding right back in on us. Won't it?"

"I wish I could promise it, Annie, that somehow we won't let all that bullshit wear us down—but I know it's going to. We have to keep recreating it, over and over, or we lose it. It happens to me every time I'm apart from you for too long. I start forgetting this feeling. I start explaining it away. I *think* about it. I *talk* about it. I do everything but *feel* it. No wonder I've been so confused. I've been looking in the wrong place. Annie, listen to me. I love you with all my heart and all my soul. Please never doubt it again."

She wiped fresh tears from her eyes. "I promise, I won't. And I promise, I won't ever let you doubt yourself again either, sweetheart. I love you too."

The effective sex scene is not about sex. It's about passion. It's about what you're looking for when you search other people's faces—you're looking for someone who will be just as delighted to look back into *your* eyes.

Love Scenes

*Anyone can write a sex scene. It takes
a real artist to write a love scene.*

A love scene is *not* about sex. A love scene isn't even about *love*.

It's about *the relationship*.

It is about the place where love occurs.

Most people—and I say this fully cognizant that most people will disagree—but most people do not know what love is.

Yes, most people have experienced love. In fact, it would be pretty tragic if they had *never* experienced love. But most folks don't *know* what love is. (If you ask them to explain love, you will get a demonstration of people making things up because they don't want to look stupid for not having a clear answer.)

And even though most people will probably regard love as the greatest of all emotions, few of them will ever take the time to find out what it takes to attain a loving relationship. We take it for granted that we already know how to love—and that's why it eludes us.

Heinlein wrote, in *Stranger in a Strange Land*, that "love is that condition where the other person's happiness is essential to your own," and that's a pretty good definition, as far as it goes.

I don't think it goes far enough. For one thing, that description could just as easily apply to altruism, which is related to love, but it isn't *really* love.

A relationship of love contains affection, trust, respect, honesty, playfulness, and commitment. All are parts of the relationship. (And probably a whole bunch of other stuff too, but these are the ones that are obvious to me.)

A love scene is a scene in which the love between two characters is *demonstrated*. It must show all of the things listed above: *affection, trust, respect, honesty, playfulness, and commitment.* But even that is not all there is to a love scene.

A love scene occurs whenever two people complete their relationship—whenever they say everything they have to say to each other and there is nothing left unsaid.

Of all the things that two people have to say to each other, *"I love you"* is one of the nicest. But it doesn't always have to be said. It isn't essential to a love scene because it's already there—it is the emotional *context* of the scene. Yes, it's nice to say it, and it's even nicer to hear, but it isn't always necessary. And indeed, sometimes it's even inappropriate—but the presence of it doesn't make a love scene, and the lack of it doesn't negate a love scene.

By the way, a love scene is not always a scene between lovers. In fact, most of the time it *isn't*. A love scene is between two people who love each other: parent and child, brother and sister, grandparent and grandchild, friend and friend, colleague and colleague, uncle and nephew, teacher and student, and so on. Any time that two people create a relationship of affection, trust, honesty, respect, playfulness, and commitment to each other, they have achieved a profound relationship; *love* is the only appropriate word.

Here is a love scene from *A Method for Madness*. (Not yet published at the time of this writing.)

> "Hey—?" Lizard asked abruptly. "What's a *gimtree?*"

"Don't you know?"

"It's your word. Not mine."

"It was named after the famous American flimflam man," I said. "Elmer Gimtree."

She phrased her next words carefully, "Before you go on, I feel I should remind you that the perfect pun always results in the death of the perpetrator. You're on dangerous ground here."

"I'm not scared. A good pun is its own reword."

"Uh-huh. And the beauty of a pun is in the *oy* of the beholder."

"And the shortest distance between two puns—"

"—*is a straight line!*" we both finished together.

"I liked the limericks better," she said. "Puns are like farts. I don't mind you enjoying your own, but you really don't have to share the experience. Now who's Elmer Gimtree?"

"You honestly don't know?" I asked in mock surprise, facing her directly. "Elmer Gimtree was world-famous for making up the most outrageous stories on the spur of the moment."

"Never heard of him," she said. She raised herself up on one elbow; she raised one eyebrow expectantly. "This had better be good, McCarthy."

"Elmer Gimtree was my dad's alter ego," I explained. "Whenever we asked him a question, he always made up a weird story. Like once when I was eight or nine, I asked him what all the weird buttons were on the dashboard of the car. Without missing a beat, he started explaining them. 'This one is the passenger-ejector-seat button. This one fires the machine guns. This one activates the antivehicular missile defense. And this one leaves an oil slick for pursuing cars to skid out on.' And my sister and I would always try to trip him up. I'd ask, 'How come you don't have a button for the grinder that comes out of the axle and slices up the tires of the car next to you?' And he'd always have an answer. He'd say, 'Oh, that cost too much extra' or something like that. So a gimtree is any really great, really silly story."

"And this is the man I want for the father of my baby?" she asked dryly. "But why do you call it a gimtree?"

"Because once I asked him why the drink was called a vodka gimlet . . . and he said it was made with vodka and gimberries. And the gimberries . . ."

". . . Come from the *gimtree*. I got it."

"So from that time on, all his stories were gimtrees. And he was Elmer Gimtree, the storyteller."

"I love it," she said. "Your family must have been crazy."

"We weren't certifiable," I said. "But we had our good moments. Once . . . on Thanksgiving, we had at least a dozen guests—and my mom dropped the turkey. She started to cry. Dad got up from the table, helped her put it back on the platter, and told her to take it back into the kitchen and get the *other* turkey. He was fast that way. He was amazing sometimes."

She smiled silently. And I didn't add anything else. I was remembering some of the other stuff, some of the stuff that hadn't been as much fun. I couldn't blame my parents for their mistakes. Everybody figures out how to be a parent in their own turn; everybody tries not to repeat the mistakes their own parents made, and in the process, they make new ones. I'd probably do the same when our baby was born.

If we got out of here. If . . .

Lizard reached over and touched me. "Are you okay, Jim?"

"Yeah." And then I added, "You're not going to believe this—I'm thinking of chili."

"Chili?" She looked at me incredulously. "We're in the middle of the Amazon jungle, surrounded by carnivorous caterpillars from outer space—*and you're thinking about food?*"

"Not food. Chili. Really awful chili. Remember that place in California . . . The World's Worst Chili!"

"*Oh, God, yes!* Sasha Miller's Dreadful Chili." Lizard rolled over on her back, laughing. "That was the *worst* meal I ever had in my entire life. I'd rather be here than there."

"That's why I was thinking about it. I was asking myself what could be worse than this? And that's what popped into my head. Sasha Miller's chili."

"Ick." Lizard made a face. "I wish you hadn't reminded me. Now I've got that awful taste in my mouth again."

"I'm sorry. Boy, I'll be apologizing for that one for the rest of my life."

"You could have plastered a house with that crap—" Lizard groaned. "No self-respecting cockroach would touch it."

"Remember the TV commercials? The dumpy woman with the frizzy orange hair tossing weird things into a bubbling cauldron—a box of cigars, a bicycle tire, a modem, a paperback novel, a bucket of millipedes, a dead cat, you name it."

"And then she'd cackle into the camera, and she'd say—" Lizard's voice went into a gravelly imitation: " 'Are you man enough to eat my chili?' "

"And they'd show her pouring it into the fuel tank

of a space shuttle." We were both laughing now. "I thought it was all a gimmick that she advertised it as the world's worst chili—but it really *was*."

Lizard rolled on her side to smile at me. "I know why you took me there, Jim. So I'd stop complaining about your cooking."

"It worked."

"I was sick for a week," she said.

"You *farted* for a week."

"I never had chili with maraschino cherries in it before. Whatever happened to Sasha Miller anyway?"

"You didn't hear?"

"No, what?"

I clutched my side painfully. It hurt to laugh, but I couldn't help myself. "I'm sorry, I shouldn't be giggling like this, it really was tragic, but it was her own damn pigheaded fault. She went to Denver to make a commercial with one of the tame Chtorrans they had there. Well, not really tame, but you know. I don't know how she and her crew got in; they must have bribed someone. Anyway, she was there standing next to the worm, holding up a big bowl of her chili saying, 'My chili makes Chtorrans purr.' And then she offered it to the worm—she'd been warned not to—well, that Chtorran purred all right, but it wasn't about the chili. Copies of that video were all over the Net for days. If they could have figured out how to use that as a commercial, I'm sure they would have." I levered up on an elbow, still smiling. "Okay—what's so funny?"

Her expression was abruptly deadpan with wide-eyed curiosity. "Did the worm fart much?"

"It died," I said.

"It died?"

"Choked to death trying to get her all down."

That was too much. Lizard burst out laughing. "I'm sorry—I can't help it."

Neither could I. We were giddy with our own hysteria. It was everything all at once. You can only be frightened for so long and then—you can't. "It's all right," I said around my own cackles. "There were so many jokes about Sasha's chili—this was just the best one of all. I can't believe you didn't hear about it. That chili really was a fatal distraction."

Lizard held up a hand to stop me. "No more. No more. I *really am* starting to remember what that stuff tasted like. Ick. I'm going to start farting any minute now."

"You win," I said quickly.

"Let's talk about real food instead."

"Okay . . . chocolate."

"Chocolate?—Oh, you bastard! You would! Torment me, why don't you? *Ooh, I want some chocolate now.* Just the sound of the word is delicious." She licked her lips luxuriously. "Mmmm. Remember that feast on the *Bosch?* . . . Oh, what a wedding night that was. Marry me again, Jim. Just for the chocolate."

My mouth was already watering. I was suddenly uncomfortable. "This is not a good idea, Lizard. Talking about food like this."

"Yes, it is. Say chocolate again. Please? *Please, Jim?*"

I swallowed hard. "*Chocolate, chocolate, chocolate. . . .*"

"God, I *love* it when you talk dirty." Abruptly, she rolled into my arms and held me as tightly as she could. "Hold me close and talk about chocolate, Jim! Please!"

"Dark chocolate," I whispered into her beautiful left ear. "So dark it hurts. So smooth and soft, you can swim in it forever. Poured over sweet rich treasures. Luscious sweet caramel. Everlasting buttercream. And truffles so rich, even the smell is intoxicating. *Chocolate . . . all the chocolate in the world.* Chocolate raspberry truffle. Double double chocolate fudge swirl. Black forest chocolate-cherry delight. *Chocolate. . . ."*

She sobbed into my shirt, clutching it between her fingers. I stopped talking then and just held her close, stroking her back like a baby. After a bit, I felt her relax. I knew the signal. She was getting herself ready to be Lizard again. General Tirelli.

I cleared my throat gently. It still hurt. "So . . . how bad is the syndrome?" I asked. "How bad does it get?"

"You saw Guyer."

"Yeah, but . . . he was *living* in the camp. That poor bastard had been hyperassaulted by Chtorran organisms. Do you think he could ever be normal again? Could he recover if he were returned to an Earth-normal environment?"

"Nobody knows," she whispered.

"God . . ." I said. "I hope I never get like that. I can't even begin to imagine it—being so far off the deep end that you can't even tell. Sweetheart—" I shifted slightly so I could look into her troubled eyes. "If I ever end up like that, if there's no hope of recovery . . . I want to be euthanized. I don't want to be a freak. Promise me?"

She didn't answer. I knew she was still awake. And I was sure I knew why she wasn't answering. Because it was a very real possibility that I *might* end up like Guyer. Dr. John Guyer. Harvard Research Tribe. . . .

"Jim," she said.

"What?"

"You once told me to never give up hope."

"You're right."

"Are you changing your commitment?"

"To you? Never."

She didn't answer that. She rolled away for a moment, onto her back. She stared up at the top of the tent. I realized I had no idea at all what she was thinking about, but whatever it was, I could see in her eyes how deeply it troubled her. "Share it," I whispered.

"Trust me, Jim. I can't. Not yet. When we get to Luna, maybe—"

I'd seen her like this before—twice. Each time, it had been a crisis of enormous self-doubt. Each time I worried that she'd hold it in until she imploded.

"Are you scared about the baby?"

"I'm scared about everything." She angled her head around to glance out the tent flap. There was nothing to see. She rolled over on her stomach and edged forward, lifting one of the flaps to give herself a better view.

I reached over and stroked her hair. It was matted and stringy. I didn't care. "I don't think they're going to do it," I said. "If they were, they'd have done it already. I think we scared them pretty badly." Lizard took my hand, she squeezed it hard in hers. Our conversation was punctuated with little moments of affection, secret connections of hands and eyes.

"Maybe they just have to work up their courage. . . ."

"No, I don't think so. These aren't bad men. They're just scared. Terrified. They're looking for someone or something to hurt back. That's all. When they calm down, they'll have to realize. . . ."

She stopped me with a wry smile. "That's what you want to believe, isn't it?"

"Desperately," I admitted, answering her smile with one of my own.

She began nervously twisting a button on my shirt. When she spoke again, it was in that little girl voice she used when she was most frightened. "I keep thinking of Nicholas and Alexandra. They didn't believe their captors would hurt them either. What if this is our last night together, Jim?"

I didn't have anything to say to that. This conversation was suddenly too painful—because there wasn't anything I could do to change the situation. I fell back in despair and studied the roof of the tent with her.

"If this really is our last night of life," I began slowly. "Let's not waste it. Let's fill another cup of happiness."

"I don't know if I can—" she choked on her words.

"Try," I insisted, rolling over to face her again. "What makes you happy? More chocolate?"

She shook her head silently, with just the barest brushing of her crimson hair against my cheek.

I waited. I stroked her neck. I put my hand on the hollow place below her throat, it was painfully smooth. I let my fingers trace their way up to her cheek. It was wet. I wiped the tears away with my thumb. "Go on," I said. "*That* one—say it."

"Mrs. McCarthy. . . ." she whispered, almost with embarrassment.

"I like the sound of that," I agreed. "It gives me a heart-on."

"A hard-on? Here? Now?"

"No. A *heart-on.* That's when your heart is so happy, you can feel it all over."

"Oh," she said, getting it. "That's nice. I like that." Then she added, "I like being a wife again. I like *belonging* to someone. I like being your wife."

"Mm. I've never been a wife. I hope it's as nice as being a husband."

"It's funny . . ." She pulled back to look at me in the darkness. She ran her fingers gently through my hair. "I never thought I'd ever get married again. And I certainly didn't imagine when we started out. . . ."

"Me neither. . . ."

"But I'm glad."

"So am I."

"Here," she said. "Let's get comfortable. . . ."

"I *am* comfortable—"

"Shh."

My dear wife pushed me back down so she could pull the mylar heating-blanket over the both of us. Then she curled up next to me again, as close as she could without hurting my leg. "Right now," she said softly, "all I want to do is lay here next to you, holding you tight with the covers pulled up over our heads. Let's pretend we're only seven years old and we're camping out in the back yard, whispering silly secrets, and the whole rest of the world just doesn't exist anymore. Okay? Please?"

I murmured assent. I knew what she was really asking.

Maybe the worms would find us. Maybe Salcido or Kruger would kill us for our share of the supplies— or just to keep us quiet. In the face of such uncertainty, there was nothing else we could do but have our honeymoon. We needed each other's strength.

Painfully, I turned on my side to face her. "I love you, sweetheart," I said. "More than life itself."

"And I love you too. More than you know." She kissed me gently. Deliciously. It was a curious moment for both of us. We were so in love with each other—and sex had nothing to do with it at all.

"I was so worried about you," she said. "The whole time I was trapped in the wreckage of the *Bosch*, all I could think of was you and what you must have been going through, not knowing and all. I felt so awful. And then . . . " her voice cracked, " . . . and then, after all that time waiting, I heard noises. At first, I thought it was rescuers, I *prayed* that it was, but then I realized it was a—a worm." She stopped abruptly. Her throat was too tight for her to continue. She started shaking. The memories were too real, too painful for her to revisit.

I held her delicately in my arms and waited patiently while she sobbed into my chest. I stroked her hair. "It's all right," I said. "You don't have to. . . ."

"No, I do," she insisted, weakly. "You have to know. I want you to hear this." She found her voice again, a hoarse whisper now. "I was so scared. I thought I was going to die. And then I remembered the promise—remember the promise that I asked you to make?"

I nodded uncomfortably, holding her close. In the darkness, my unshaven cheek brushed roughly against the smooth skin of her neck.

It wasn't enough. She had to hear me say it aloud. "*Remember*, Jim?" Her voice was intense. Her fingers clutched my shirt, bunching up the fabric in a painful knot.

"I remember," I said, not remembering at all—we

had made so many promises to each other. I wondered where this conversation was heading. I wished we could just lie still instead.

But, no. This was too important to her. "I asked you to promise me that you'd never let me be eaten by a worm—" she reminded desperately.

Oh. *That* promise. It had been an easy one to make. I'd never believed I'd ever have to keep it. We'd come so very far in such a short time. Now I wondered how I'd be able to keep it without even a stick to throw at a worm.

"—While I was trapped there in that wreckage, I knew that you weren't going to save me. I could hear this big worm making those horrible churpling noises, chewing its way through the walls. It was pulling everything apart, looking for things to eat. I knew it was going to find me and kill me—*I knew it, Jim*—and I knew that you'd never forgive yourself afterward for not being able to keep your promise. And that's when I knew I had to find a way to live, because I had to tell you I was wrong to ask you to promise such a thing. Because it wasn't fair." She clutched me hard. Her eyes bored deep into mine. "You have to make me a new promise, Jim. A better one—"

"*Anything*, my love. Anything you want."

"No, listen." She sounded frantic now. "Promise me this. Whatever happens—*whatever*—promise me that you'll forgive yourself afterwards."

"I don't understand . . . what you're asking."

"Promise me that you'll forgive yourself. That's all. Please?" She sounded desperate. Her fingers dug into my arm.

I tried to pull her closer, tried to comfort her. I tried to sound as sincere as I could, even though I still didn't get it. "I promise," I said. "You can count on me. No matter what happens, I'll apologize to me as best as I can, and then I'll forgive myself. Okay?" I didn't know if I sounded sincere or silly.

"Jim, *please!*"

Too silly. I tried again. "Cross my heart and hope to die." I felt exactly like a seven-year-old. What else could I say to her?

"Stick a noodle in your eye? . . ." she asked.

"I think that's supposed to be *needle.*"

"Yes, I know," she whispered softly, "but I don't want you hurting yourself."

"Lover, I promise you. I won't hurt myself. And I'll keep my promise."

She relaxed in my arms. "Good," she said. At last, she sounded satisfied. "Thank you." She sighed and snuggled up safely again, making little moaning sounds of comfort. She changed the subject incongruously. "This isn't exactly the honeymoon we'd planned, but I'm happy."

"Me too."

Yes, it's long. But it could be the last time that these two characters will have any private time together. I decided to just let them talk and see where they would go. Considering what they've been through, they've earned it.

Maybe someday I'll edit it down.

But probably not.

Sentences

First say it aloud. If it's hard to say,
don't type it. It'll be just as hard to read.

A sentence is a thought. A paragraph is a collection of thoughts. The way you construct your sentences and your paragraphs is a representation of your thought processes. If your thinking is clear, your sentences will be effective. If your thinking is confused, your sentences will be confused.

If you find yourself fumbling around for the right words, it means you don't have a clear image in your mind. Stop and visualize what it is you want to evoke.

Visualize first, then describe. Short sentences work best. Short sentences provide clarity and a crisp readable style. Short sentences create a rapid staccato feeling. This is very useful for writing action. Ernest Hemingway was known for using short simple sentences. It gave his work immediacy. He is still regarded as one of the greatest American authors.

Long and involved sentences must be approached with caution, because they can grow quickly out of control, dragging the writer's thought processes into tangled thickets of verbiage from which there may be no clear escape, leaving the reader stranded without a machete inside a dense jungle of metaphor. If you are describing a cascade of emotion and action where many things are happening rapidly, one after the other, a long tumbling sentence can help to create a flowing sensation of motion; but you will usually find that clarity is heightened by breaking long flowing sentences into their component parts so that each specific thought gets its own sentence and receives appropriate attention.

Eventually, after you have constructed your first million paragraphs, you will find that you can think in both long and short sentences. You will establish a rhythm in your paragraphs—alternating the long and the short to point up specific thoughts.

Simile

Similes are as easy as falling off a bicycle.
You never forget how.

A simile is a comparison—usually a surprising one.

It is any phrase in which something is compared to something else. You can usually identify a simile because it uses the word *like* or *as* to introduce a comparison.

Similes can be as useful as a magnifying glass—or they can be as tangential and inappropriate as pliers at the dinner table.

> The starship looked clunky—as if someone had dumped a junkyard into a giant bag and shaken it thoroughly.

> She was as graceful as a cat—if a cat weighed four hundred pounds and had six legs and two swollen udders.

> As magical as a Tuesday morning in Summer school.

> Maizlish had an astonishing nose. If a fat, warty, green pickle had climbed out of the barrel and fastened itself onto his face, it wouldn't have looked as out of place.

Similes are like garlic. They should be used sparingly. Otherwise, they leave a terrible taste in the mouth.

A bad simile is as ludicrous as a wrestler in a tutu—and even an effective simile calls attention to itself. You don't want to pull the reader out of the flow of the story, but that's exactly what similes do—they introduce new and often *discordant* images.

Sometimes that's useful because sometimes that's exactly what you want to do—the simile is the voice of the narrator or even the author's own sly comment on events.

Metaphor

A man's speech should exceed his grasp,
or what's a metaphor?

Metaphors are wonderful creatures. They can sail into star-lit skies, they can burrow into dark, decaying dungeons, they can stride across the mountaintops, they can creep underneath your fingernails.

A metaphor is a game of pretend.

When you pretend, you put on some makeup, a wig, a funny hat, a costume, and you take on the flavor of that thing you are pretending to be. So it is with metaphors.

A metaphor pretends that something is something else. And by that pretense, that person, place, or thing takes on the desired characteristics.

> The old bus coughed. It heaved a final painful rattle. It sagged and died. Behind it, the cars began to growl.

> Harry's dignity gathered up its skirts and left in a huff, leaving Harry behind, gasping, red-faced, and embarrassed.

> Leonard was a walking elbow-wrinkle of a man. He was eight pounds of potatoes in a ten-pound sack.

> Robbins reeked—mostly with the pheromones of money.

A metaphor is a one-sentence fantasy. It assigns lifelike or magical qualities to ordinary objects. Metaphor and fantasy are bedfellows—and many fantasies are intended as metaphors; George Orwell's *Animal Farm* is the best example of this.

Be careful with metaphors. *Don't overuse* metaphors. Sometimes they take on lives of their own and run away with your best intentions, turning your story into something that is neither fish nor fowl, that neither swims nor flies but flaps helplessly around, splashing and quacking, and leaves the reader shaking his head and wondering what kind of beast the author is trying to manage.

Beware of *mixing metaphors*, lest you end up with a menagerie of strange creatures staring quizzically at each other across the chasms of disbelief: a mishmash of verbal zoology, an island of Dr. Moreau's chimerical creatures of language, producing a violent clashing of the machinery of meaning—bubbling and fuming and erupting in stylistic disaster.

If a simile is garlic, then a metaphor is chili powder. Enhance the story, don't overwhelm it.

Adjectives and Adverbs

*A little makeup accentuates your best
qualities—but put on too much makeup
and you look like a clown. Adjectives
work the same way.*

Adjectives and adverbs are modifiers. They *change* the
meanings of the words they are attached to.

The dog in the car barked.

The big dog in the red car barked wildly.

The big shaggy dog in the bright red car barked wildly
and frantically.

The big, white, shaggy dog in the shining bright red car
barked wildly and frantically and enthusiastically.

A sentence can only carry so much weight. Too much
is way too much. Stop before your sentence collapses like
a sick soufflé. Remember Hemingway? He used adjectives
like a miser—as if he were paying ten bucks apiece for them.
In science fiction and fantasy, you are describing things
that are beyond the reader's experience—they are also beyond *your* experience—so the job of evoking person, place,

and thing is made more difficult; but overloading the description with adjectives does not clarify the experience, it muddies it. This kind of writing usually occurs when the writer doesn't have a clear sense of what he's describing, so—like someone who cooks by ear—he pours into the pot every spice in the cabinet.

Here's the cure. First visualize the scene as if it's right in front of you. Imagine what it would look like if a great film director were to put it on screen. Then say what it feels like. Yes, you can still use adjectives, but when you use them sparingly, each one has far more impact:

> The black-cloaked figure waited silently at the end of the path.

> Jupiter filled the western sky like a vast orange wall.

> Impatient to eat, the giant insect clacked its mandibles.

> Grass—an endless sea of grass—rolled out to the horizon. Waves of shadow rippled beneath the wind.

> The knight was sultry. She bent her knee and bowed to the prince.

Finding the
Right Words

---

*"The difference between the right word and the
almost-right word is the difference between
lightning and a lightning bug."*—Mark Twain

Your goal is to create surprises in every sentence. This
means that you must find ways to startle the reader with
moments of recognition and delight—especially with
cheap shots:

> Lennie the lawyer slouched in. "Hello," he lied.

> She dressed like a fashion-crime looking for a place
> to happen.

> "I'm sorry," the redhead said. "But I don't date out-
> side my species."

> Lennie was the kind of guy who had to remind himself
> "yellow in front, brown in back" before putting on
> his underwear.

> The sergeant stopped me before I could ask my ques-
> tion. "Shut up!" he explained.

> "No, I'm not interested in your sexual orientation,

and no, I don't want to know the name of your sheep."

She could turn parts of men to stone just by looking at them.

She rubbed her hand up my chest and said very eloquently, "*Mmmmmmmmmmm.*"

Occasionally, you may feel the need to make up a new word. Be careful. Sometimes you can do this to great effect, but not always.

The best example occurs in Robert A. Heinlein's brilliant novel, *Stranger in a Strange Land.* Valentine Michael Smith, raised by Martians, returns to Earth, not knowing how to be human. He puzzles over the simplest things. He does not yet *grok* humanity.

What does *grok* mean?

In Martian, it means *drink.* But it also means to drink *deeply.* It means to drink the moment so deeply that it becomes part of who you are. It means to *get* it. Understanding something comes from reading about it, but grokking comes from doing.

When you are writing science fiction or fantasy, you will always be tempted to make up new words—especially technical-sounding terms like quadro-triticale and veeble-fetzer. Be careful. Techno-jargon is like *bolognium*: One piece too many and everything implodes.

As a general rule, you should always be wary of inventing new words. Be *abscemious*, not *obstential.*

He *mrmfled* around a mouthful of sandwich.

"You know what you are? You're a *buttersnipe.* Someone so sweet and nice that butter wouldn't melt in her mouth—even while she's saying some very nasty and hurtful things."

The fat woman *flubbered* into the room.

The rabbits chewed their way out of the hutch and escaped into the woods behind the house, where they *tribbled* happily for several generations.

In other words, don't show off . . . *at least not unless the risk is worth it.*

Paragraphs

The moving finger writes, and having writ,
then goes back and rewrites and rewrites
and rewrites. . . .

Your story exists as a series of paragraphs.

Each paragraph is a complete moment. Every sentence in the paragraph is part of the moment, a necessary component to the whole. When you've said everything you have to say about that specific moment, end the paragraph and start the next. It's that simple.

A paragraph must accomplish two things. First, it must evoke the specific moment you want to create. Second, it must kick the reader into the next paragraph—where the next moment will occur. If a paragraph doesn't accomplish either, then why did you write it?

A successful paragraph will evoke action, emotion, and the physical senses. You want to tell not only what happens but also what it feels like. (This is the lesson I learned from Poul Anderson.) To make your writing vivid, you must engage all the senses. Evoke the colors, the sounds, the smells, the tastes, and all the physical sensations.

Here are the questions that you want to answer in an effective paragraph:

- What is this moment about? What's happening here? What does it look like?
- What visual image do I want to create? What do the other senses report?

- What is the visceral feeling? What is the emotion? The mood?

Suppose you're writing a paragraph in which an astronaut steps out onto the surface of the moon. For the purposes of your story, the point you need to make is how dark and barren the lunar landscape looks. You have to create a *visual* sense of a lifeless, airless, empty terrain, a visceral *feeling* of loneliness and desolation, and a *sense* that your astronaut feels triumph and awe.

Tucker took the last step off the bottom rung of the ladder. His booted foot sank into the soft powdery surface. First one, then the other. He let go of the ladder, then turned around slowly, taking it all in.

The ground rolled unevenly out to an impossibly close horizon. The sun glared bright and low in the sky behind him, outlining everything with long harsh shadows. Ahead, silvery boulders shone bright beneath the strange black daylight sky; they lay across the pocked and cratered landscape, as if strewn from a giant's toy box.

The sound of his own breathing filled his helmet. He could hear the rushing of the blood in his ears, and the energized pumping of his heart. The air in his spacesuit tasted metallic. He smelled his own sweat. None of it mattered—he was standing on the moon! At last! He looked up at the big blue marble of Earth. It glowed like an enchanted gemstone.

He felt very small and far away, and at the same time he felt so proud he had no words. His eyes grew moist with emotion. *We were back!*

Notice how, as you go through the paragraphs, each of the questions is answered in turn.

Now let's try it again, this time in a fantasy story. A human child is alone in a strange forest. She meets an enchanted dragon who will become her friend. We want to make the point that the dragon appears huge and dangerous and powerful. We want to evoke an *image* of strength and hunger, a *feeling* of awe and fear, and a *sense* of curiosity:

> Disoriented, Arianne slipped and stumbled through the dark forest—and slid unexpectedly down a grassy slope into a bright clearing that tasted of sunlight.
>
> She wasn't alone here. A giant wall of glittering yellow—she had tumbled into it—rose up in front of her. It moved! It stretched itself up mightily—and suddenly a giant orange head came swinging majestically around. Black bottomless eyes, as big as wagon wheels, blinked and focused on her.
>
> It was the golden dragon! The same one she'd seen before, splashing in the sea! It smelled of salt and copper and the deep dark earth. The dragon gazed down at her with unblinking eyes. It looked as wise as time.
>
> The dragon opened its mouth and its breath came hot—as hot as the blast of a furnace. In terror, Arianne scrambled for her shield—the shield the wizard had given her. She held it high against the fire to come.
>
> The silver crest glittered and caught the sunlight, flashing into the eyes of the beast.
>
> The dragon paused. Its long exhalation finished, it now inhaled several days of air.
>
> Did it study her? Arianne took a step back, uncertainly . . . she was too awestruck to run, her legs

felt like jelly, but if the dragon intended to kill her, surely it would have done so already. Had it recognized the shield? She lowered it, peering curiously over the top.

The dragon opened its wings to their full length, as if readying itself to leap into the air—but it was only stretching. It furled its wings again, then lowered its great head to the ground and rumbled deep within its chest, a long and painful moan of grief. The forest resonated with the dreadful sound.

Notice how each of the questions gets answered in turn. To the extent that you can evoke the *image*, the *feeling*, and the *mood*, your paragraphs will work.

A word of caution. Take care with your descriptions. Beware of clichés and anachronisms. For instance, a dragon cannot have a wingspread as wide as a football field—because football does not exist in the medieval world of dragons and wizards. Don't do this:

The dwarf looked like something out of a Spielberg movie. He was only as tall as a fire hydrant, but he struck sparks off his sword like a welder's torch. His eyes shone red as lasers, his voice rasped like Darth Vader's. The king's guards looked at him like a SWAT team studying a hostage-taker.

The writing voice in that paragraph is firmly rooted in contemporary America. The only justification for such a tone would be if the dwarf had fallen out of the sky into the bedroom of a slightly misanthropic adolescent who spent too much time watching television.

Better to do this:

> The dwarf was clearly from a distant land—his look, his manner, his style of dress. Barely as tall as his shield, his sword glimmered like the reflection of fireflies in water. His eyes smoldered. His voice rasped. The king's men studied him warily.

Notice that the second description depends much less on simile and much more on simple evocation.

Use your descriptions to evoke not just the moment but also the world in which the moment occurs. That's why the dragon's eyes aren't as big as portholes, they're as big as wagon wheels—because that's how Arianne knows the world she lives in.

And that's how the reader will know it too.

Evoking

Here's another trick.

Suppose you want a paragraph to suggest something magical and moody—like the dark center of a forest where enchantment lurks.

Make a list of all the words that will evoke the feeling of this forest:

> cold
> sparkling leaves
> gnarled
> dark
> twisted tree trunks
> luminous
> moonlight
> silence
> white wolves
> gliding

Now try to see how many of these words or images you can use in a paragraph. Don't overdo it. You don't have to use them all.

> The gnarled trees crouched beneath the luminous night. Branches twisted toward the cold sky like clutching fingers reaching for the first soft flakes of snow. In the clearing, the white wolves gathered si-

lently as ghosts. The moonlit ground glistened with the frozen breath of winter.

Notice there are only four thoughts in this paragraph. The first and second sentences set the scene. The third sentence tells you what is happening, and the fourth sentence adds one more piece of description.

Remember your high school English course? Remember how your teacher tried to explain to you that every paragraph has a *theme sentence?* When you're telling a story, every paragraph should have one sentence that advances the story to the next paragraph. In this paragraph the white wolves are gathering. In the next paragraph, the *next* event occurs:

> The leader of the pack lifted his nose to the wind. There was *something* out there—something *unfamiliar*. To the east? . . . Memories of pain. Something unpleasant in that realm.

And in the *next* paragraph, the *next* event occurs:

> Yes, to the east.
> He had the scent now. Whatever the acrid memories, he was stronger now. And *hungrier*. Like a wraith, he moved softly out of the glade. The others followed after, their paws light upon the glassy surface of the snow.

Notice that every moment of action is also an opportunity to add another sentence of description—another piece of the overall picture.

Here's something else to remember. Don't overuse the same word in a series of paragraphs. Try to find other words that expand the meaning. For instance, Edgar Allan Poe never used the word "room" when he could also use *chambers, apartment, quarters, lodging, accommodation, domicile, berth, billet, board, bed, structure, building,* or *harbor.*[18] As well as *dungeon, prison, cell,* and *habitation.*

[18] *The Pit and the Pendulum*, by Edgar Allan Poe.

Metric Prose

If it's got a good beat, you can dance to it.

Midway through the seventies, Harlan Ellison hosted a lecture series at UCLA called "Ten Tuesdays Down a Rabbit Hole." Many of the science fiction writers in Los Angeles came in as guest speakers, but even on the nights they weren't speaking, many of them attended just for the fun of participating.

Theodore Sturgeon was one of those who showed up for all ten sessions. Afterward, several of us would gather at Ship's (a landmark coffee shop, long since torn down) for munchies and conversation. Some of those late night sessions became part of local legend. (Like the time I tried to strangle Wina because she wouldn't take the hint and shut up, but that's another story.)

During his lifetime, Theodore Sturgeon became the most reprinted living author in the English language. His short stories included such classics as "The Silken-Swift," "A Saucer of Loneliness," "The Comedian's Children," "Poor Superman," "Affair With a Green Monkey," "The World Well Lost," and "Microcosmic God." His landmark novel, *More Than Human*, despite its title, was the most passionately human science fiction novel of the century. (He also wrote the "Shore Leave" and "Amok Time" episodes of *Star Trek*, but those were pale intimations of what he was really capable of.) A new work by Sturgeon was always a cause for celebration.

Sturgeon was not only a remarkable stylist, he was a

remarkable human being with a rare and powerful insight into the way things worked. He was joyous and candid about the lessons he'd learned, so one night, without any embarrassment, I turned to him and asked him about *style*.

What is style, I asked. How does it work? How do you master it? I admitted that this was the one part of writing that still felt like a mystery. How do you write in a *style*?

Ted was both surprised and delighted. Nobody had ever asked him this question before, and this was a discovery that he was happy to share.

"Metric prose," he said. He pulled out a pen and started drawing on a napkin. "Language has rhythm. If you write a paragraph with a specific poetic rhythm, the reader hears that rhythm in his head as he reads, and that rhythm helps create the mood of the story. If you suddenly shift the rhythm, you shift the mood, and it's like sliding from silk onto sandpaper." He drew dashes and half-circles to illustrate the way poets mark the beats of their poems:

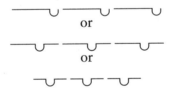

"If you continue the rhythm from one sentence to the next without missing a beat, the language flows and carries the reader along. Sometimes, to keep to the beat, you have to find different words or different ways of phrasing what you want to say, and this forces you to stretch your writing muscles."

Ted shared a few examples, and we talked about "metric prose" for the better part of an hour, oblivious to all the other discussions going on around us. He also said, impishly, that the one time he'd shared this with Frederik Pohl, his editor at *Galaxy Science Fiction* magazine, Fred had pooh-poohed it. A few years later, as Ted told it, Fred had praised "Bianca's Hands," one of Ted's most famous stories, singling out one particular paragraph as an example of great writing. Ted's eyes twinkled as he related. "Of course, that was the paragraph I'd written in metric prose."

I was fascinated. I'd never seen or heard of metric prose before. (I'd never studied poetry.) I could hardly wait to get home and start typing. The next day, I went to the closest bookstore and spent a hundred dollars on books about how to write poetry.

Over the next few years, I experimented with metric prose constantly, in almost everything I wrote. Sturgeon was right. It was a brilliant and effective way to use language—and the best part was that it did force me to think outside my usual boundaries.

She worked the soil angrily. Her face was black with grime, dark sweat rolled off her brow. The blisters on her hands were raw and would need tending soon. Aching, stretching, straightening in the heat, her back constricting and complaining, she paused to wipe her forehead. She looked across the fields. A mistake—the deadly trees still loomed. Unbidden anguish came rising out of memory.

She couldn't shut it out. It overwhelmed and toppled her. She fell. Her knees gave way. Her heart. Her eyes. "Oh, God!" she choked. "This isn't right! He didn't deserve it!" Sobbing, she pounded the earth. "Why did you take him? Answer me, God—I need an answer, now!"

Only the silence of the day. The heat of the sun. And nothing more. No answer came.

Collapsed in grief, sprawled across the dirt, her body wracked with sobs. She lay upon the bosom of the earth, uncomforted—slowly, slowly realizing that no end would come like this—not while she lay unmoving.

And she knew the answer anyway. She'd have to take her axe to the leviathan, the emperor of trees—and all the rest as well. It would be an ugly job, all summer long, a week at least for just the king—

The tenants slept in day. They would be torpid. She stood, breathing with a hard resolve. *Do it now!* She took the ax from the wagon. And headed for the trees.

She looked up once, then took her stand. *And now!* She swung the mighty ax around! It *thunked* into the leaden trunk. She jerked it loose and swung again. Around around again! Again! *Ka-thunk-a-thunk!*

No more monsters harbored here, she swore. She'd have the whole grove flat before the autumn came. They'd keep her hearth and soul warm all winter long—

Can you tell where the rhythm changed? Can you tell where it changed again? Again?

OK, I admit it—I wrote this example a little heavy-handedly. I wanted the rhythm obvious. But in your own work, you will want to experiment with different rhythms for different styles and different effects. Some will feel comfortable to you, and some will not. Use what works.

Ideally, you want each sentence to propel the reader forward to the next. Metric prose accomplishes this by establishing a rhythm. The reader might not know it, but he hears the rhythm as he reads, and his need to have the rhythm continue keeps him reading.

You don't need every paragraph to have poetic meter. You should use it for effect. Don't overwhelm the reader. If everything is high effect, then what will you do when you *really* need to make an impact?

Memes

"Eureka!" is the most dangerous
word in the world.

(*This is the bonus chapter. It's intended for advanced students only. If you aren't interested in digging under the foundations of storytelling, you can skip it.*)

Suddenly, I was sensitized to language and the way it conveyed not just meaning but mood as well.

In one of the communication workshops I took (also as a result of Theodore Sturgeon's advice), the point was driven home in a startling way: "You are a creature of language. You exist in language. Every experience you will ever feel gets conceptualized immediately in language, and every subsequent experience gets filtered through the concepts you're already carrying around. To the extent that you are unconscious of the power of language, it drives you—and most of you are comatose." During the sessions of that course, several of the exercises drove that point home like a nuclear-powered jackhammer.

Most of us are willing to agree that language creates and shapes and empowers our perceptions, but that's only the timid tip of the iceberg. The terrifying truth is that we *are our language.*

We do not conceptualize *except* through language. And not just spoken and written languages—all languages. Mathematics is a language, musical notation is a language, Ameslan is a language, BASIC is a language. All of these are conceptualizations to channel specific kinds of thinking.

Language channels thought so completely that we *cannot think except through language.*

We do not exist as rational, self-aware entities *except as we can express it through language.* Our relationship with the tool of language is symbiotic—we use it to communicate, it uses us. Language is a metameme—it is the environment in which all other memes exist.

(A *meme* is an idea, a way of thinking, that spreads through a society like a virus through a population. Strong memes drive out weaker memes. For instance, democracy is the idea that government is accountable to the people. In the eighteenth century, that meme challenged the existing paradigm of monarchy. "The consent of the governed" was a much more powerful meme than "the divine right of kings." That was the philosophical justification for the American Revolution; it was a meme successful enough to trigger the creation of a new kind of nation. Other memes include Christianity, evolution, ecology, science fiction. . . .)

We are carriers of language. We exist so much in the domain of language that we *become* our language. We cannot define ourselves except through language—and when our language-identity is threatened, we jump to defend it much quicker than we leap to defend our actual *selves.*

For instance, if you challenge someone's faith, they are likely to hold up their holy book as evidence of *the word of God.* What is that book? It's *language.* Language written down. A body of conceptualizations—codified, frozen, completed. An *unchanging* and *absolute* system of thought. To the person who regards that meme as the defining ground of being for his identity, that book *is* the word of God. There is no other place for that person to go for a sense of identity.

What this means is that if you exist within a system of logic, if you exist within a system of belief, *it is true for you*. You cannot know if it is not true. Only if you can set it aside and look at it from a *different* perspective, a different way of being, can you recognize it as a superstition.

By the way, such a step outside of oneself is usually recognized as . . . *a transformation*.

This is another way to understand what happens to the hero of your story—he shifts to a different way of being, because he moves to a different way of thinking, because he shifts to a different set of language.

Example: when the women's movement first began suggesting that words like *chairman* and *spokesman* were sexist, many people laughed at the outrageousness of the assertion. When the word *Ms.* was created as an alternative to *Miss*, some folks thought that an extreme reaction. But over time, the idea sunk in, and we started using words like *chairperson*, *spokesperson*, and *congresscritter* as substitutes. *Ms.* very quickly became the appropriate honorific for addressing women.

Any political effort to shift the language is an acknowledgment of the power of language to influence attitude. In the case of the women's movement, the shift in language is part of an ongoing cultural transformation—not just for women who felt oppressed by the inherited sexism of the English language, but also for men who had taken that tradition of privilege for granted.

Any such shift is a transformation. And all transformation is a function of language—it is the shift from "I *can't* handle this" to "I *can* handle this." It occurs *in* language.

The writer lives in language to a much greater degree than most other people. The more the writer works, the more the writer discovers the power of language. Eventually, a writer's relationship with language can become so profound that it transforms the individual. The writer shifts from the domain of the student to the domain of mastery.

Oops. There's another meme. Mastery.

What is *mastery* anyway?

To most of us, the concept is alien because we don't have many areas in our lives where we actually experience mastery. The movies tell us that a master is infinitely wise— and also a martial arts expert. Of course, we can understand the martial arts part—that's where you learn the critical move of the weeping crane or the flying buffalo, and you defeat the bully in the last reel. It's the wisdom part that eludes us.

And that has to do with the way we are educated.

Much of what we call education isn't education at all, it's memorization. Somebody stands in front of a room and talks. You sit in your chair and copy down as much of what the instructor says as you can, as fast as you can. At the end of the semester, you reread everything you've written, cramming it back into your brain. Then you go back to the classroom, pull out a blank piece of paper, and regurgitate as much as you can as fast as you can. When you're done, you walk out of the room and quickly forget everything, because the semester is over and you don't need to remember it anymore.

This is not education; this is *bulimia.*

Real education isn't about cramming and vomiting information. Real education is about distinguishing distinctions.

What's a distinction?

A distinction is a way of relating one thing to another. The simplest way to understand a distinction is to imagine it as a dividing line that distinguishes *this* from *that.* For instance, this big plastic container is filled with garbage. But if we start sorting through it and pulling out the plastic, the cardboard, the newspaper, the glass, and the metal, it's no longer *garbage* at all—now they're *recyclables.* We have distinguished each kind of refuse into a specific category.

Here's another example. Eskimos are said to have 37 different words for snow. There's new snow, old snow, very old snow, wet snow, dry snow, deep snow, snow with a crust, yellow snow . . . and so on. We only have one word for snow. Of course, an Eskimo *needs* 37 different distinctions by which to distinguish the environment. Survival depends on it.

Bring an Eskimo to southern California and he will be equally out of place. We have 37 different words for green. We have 137 different words for automobile. We have dictionaries full of words for distinguishing parts of the body and things that can go wrong. In fact, the English language has more words *and more distinctions* than any other language in the world. That's why it is the most powerful language in the world—because English gives you conceptualizations that don't exist in other languages. *If there is no word in a language for something, you can't talk about it*—at least not until you make up a word and get other people to understand your definition. That's how memes are created and spread. Relativity, for instance, was once a meme that only twelve people in the world understood. Now, it is commonly taught in high schools.

A meme is an iceberg in the sea of knowledge. Nine-tenths of it is submerged. As it floats into warmer waters, it melts into the surrounding ocean—and the water level rises correspondingly.

Here's the meme of *distinctions*. (Let's distinguish the distinction of distinctions. . . .)

There are four kinds of distinctions: inclusion, connection, disconnection, and exclusion. It works like this: Imagine that the universe consists of **A** and **B** and **C** and **D** and **E** and **F**. . . .

The distinction of inclusion lets us specify *all*. Everything is *included*. This is the distinction of groups:

The distinction of connection lets us specify *some*. Some things are *connected* to each other. This is the distinction of partnership:

The distinction of disconnection lets us specify *not-some*. Disconnection specifies boundaries and lets us discriminate between *this* and *not this*. This is the distinction of separation:

A   B   C   D   E   F

The distinction of exclusion lets us specify *none*. Everything is *excluded*. Obliterated. Removed from consciousness. Discarded. This is the distinction of elimination:

The point of this excursion into linguistic philosophy

is to demonstrate the essential simplicity of relationships. Words are symbols. Sentences are concepts. Concepts are the levers of distinction.

The more you are in command of your own language, the more distinctions you can *include* in your worldview. The more you are conscious of, the more accurate your sense of existing relationships. The more that you can distinguish, the more effectively you can respond.

To be blunt, the more distinctions you have, the more you will be a power in your universe. Why? Because you have a greater number of tools to use, and the understanding of where they're appropriate. You will appear to others as a wise, powerful, and effective individual. The job of the master is to learn the distinctions of the craft.

Which brings me back to mastery.

What is the true distinction of *mastery?* And how do you know when you achieve mastery?

My first attempt to distinguish mastery was incomplete.

I wrote this down: "Mastery comes from the willingness to *not know.*"

That sounded good. It was even true—as far as I understood it. But that definition was insufficient. It didn't recognize or acknowledge that *skill* and *effectiveness* are also a part of mastery.

So I started looking beyond that: "The master is one who remains a student forever, even after he's surpassed his teachers." But then, if he's surpassed his teachers, who does he learn from? That was the *next* question to ask— and it was the right question to ask. (Thanks, Ted!) "The master generates the lessons himself. He generates *from* the craft. The master *creates distinctions." That* was the realization!

The master transforms the craft. Mastery transcends

craft to achieve art. And by so doing, the master demonstrates *new possibilities* to others.

Consider this: In fantasy, language is the access to magic. In the real world, language is the *source* of magic. Remember "magical thinking?" Little children, not knowing that the word is not the thing, fall into the trap of believing that the word and the thing are connected—and therefore if you can manipulate the word, you can manipulate the thing. In fantasy, this is called knowing the "true name."

Much of fantasy is based on the idea of magical thinking—that magic comes from the control of things through knowing their true names, through knowing the right spells to cast.

Here, in what we call the *real world*, we don't acknowledge the power of language to affect our thinking. We are unconscious to it—therefore we are powerless before it. But language in the hands of a master writer—whether he be a storyteller or a propagandist—is a tool for transforming a person's view of what's possible in the universe.

George Orwell made this point brilliantly in *1984*, in which the government is systematically obliterating the possibility of revolution by destroying the language in which revolution would be organized. Language is worldview. Jack Vance also explored this idea in *The Languages of Pao*. In *Stranger in a Strange Land*, Heinlein suggested that the Martians were far more enlightened than humans, specifically because their language was a more accurate map of the universe.

A writer can also submerge his reader in an alien language as a way of evoking that way of thinking. In *A Clockwork Orange*, Anthony Burgess created a new language for his ultraviolent narrator. (Alex and his droogs were real horrorshow.) Through language Burgess submerged the reader in a nightmare world. In *Davy*, Edgar Pangborn applied the same technique in the opposite direction; he submerged the reader in the language of a rural American fantasy.

When you control language, you control the way people think. If you create a new word—as Heinlein did with the word "grok"—you give them a new concept and expand the reader's worldview. If you redefine a word, you *change* the reader's worldview. You can even destroy the validity of a word by demonstrating that it is meaningless—as screenwriter Lawrence Kasdan did when he gave Yoda the immortal line, "Do or do not. There is no try." When you change the language, you change the kind of thinking that is possible.

And this is the point of this whole discourse: If you are committed to the craft of writing, committed to it the same way you are committed to taking your next breath, then your tool is language—and you must engage yourself in a never-ending exploration of its power and effectiveness. Every paragraph, every sentence, every word is an opportunity to strive for mastery.

To Be or
Naught to Be

*"Existence or nullity.
The question vexes me."*—Hamlet

The more you write, the more you become sensitized to language. You start to notice little things that occur around you: accidental puns, malaprops, mixed-up phrases. Any discussion of linguistics takes on new urgency. *Can I find something in this to help my writing?*

Many years ago, I read an article in *Time* magazine about a scholar named D. David Bourland Jr. who had eschewed the use of the verb *to be*. He had removed it from both his writing and his speaking.

Bourland felt that the verb functioned as a linguistic trap—a pitfall for the mind. According to the summary in the article, the use of the verb *to be* assigns static qualities to people, places, and things, despite the fact that people, places, and things *change*. Therefore, the use of the verb creates an inherent lie, not just in the linguistic representation of the moment, but also in the worldview of the mind that uses such constructions.

On a much less profound level, the verb *to be* seduces the unwary into writing the dreaded passive-voice sentence—a construction that troubles the sleep of editors, high school English teachers, and those who write grammar-checking software.

Therefore *to be* is *naught* to be.[19]

The folks who study general semantics call this linguistic discipline—the banishment of the existential verb—*E-Prime*. Many of them have excised the verb from their writing and their speaking. They contend that language deludes us into believing that the structural relationships of language also hold true in the physical world. The idea of *being* legitimizes and perpetuates the assumption that *things stay the same*. Abandoning it changes the logical structure of language, and therefore the logical structure of thought as well.

Passive statements obscure authorship of an event; E-Prime statements include the participant-observer. They exercise the active quality of identity. People and objects reinvent themselves as authors of their own participation.

I saved the article for future reference; it represented an intriguing exploration of language, although I didn't quite grasp it at the time. Over the years, the page would occasionally float unbidden to the top of the various stacks of unsorted stuff that populate my office. And every time it surfaced, I found myself rereading the article, and every time it tweaked my interest again.

The question vexed me.

This innocent little verb seemed one of the most essential parts of English. How could anyone write anything at all without using some form of it? A paragraph? A page? A book? It seemed impossible. The verb has rooted itself so thoroughly into the language and into the way we think that breaking out would represent a *transformative* act.

Of course, once I looked at it that way. . . .

So I asked the question again. If I could master this technique, what would I gain?

---

[19] Sorry. I couldn't resist.

According to the E-Prime evangelists, language infected with *being* has a flat and unexciting quality. Language without the obnoxious conjugations has a more active and assertive flavor. The various examples make that clear. The elimination of fixed states creates a more fluid and effective form of communication.

Here are some examples:

> The stoplight was red.
> The house is old.
> I am ugly.
> They were finished.
> He isn't coming.

Before you turn the page, try rewriting these sentences yourself to avoid the verbs of being.

Here's one way to rewrite the sample sentences:

> The stoplight had turned red.
> The house looked old.
> I feel ugly.
> They had finished.
> I forgot to tell you, Godot called. He can't make it.

Do the latter examples convey more meaning? Do they feel more lively and precise? I think they do.

Shakespeare had it right. The linguistic question of "to *be* or not to *be*" forces a confrontation with the fundamental dilemma of existence. What relationship do we really have with everything around us? What relationship do we want to create?

My resistant self wanted to argue for the verb as a necessary part of speech—I mean, how else could we discuss *existence* if we have no word for it?[20] But on the other hand, if the use of the verb did in fact represent a semantic dead end, as the E-Prime advocates claimed, then as an author committed to the expansion of my craft, I had no choice but to explore the possibility. In fact, my own integrity demanded it. I couldn't stand the *not*-knowing. I had to learn this skill.

The first time I tried writing without any form of the verb *to be*, I gave myself a frustration-tantrum that lasted four months. I had to put the book aside for two more months before I could come back to it. Eventually, I did write two long novels in E-Prime: *Under the Eye of God* and *A Covenant of Justice*. Despite my practically giving it away at the end of the second book that I had abandoned the use of the verb *to be* for these two volumes, nobody noticed. And when I did point it out to others, nobody seemed to care. Or perhaps they didn't understand the size of the challenge. Nevertheless . . . I remain proud of the effort.

I doubt I would have even attempted the challenge before the age of the word processor, because as carefully as I worked, I knew that I would still make mistakes and inadvertently or unconsciously use the verboten language. Occasionally, for instance, I fell into metric paragraphs and didn't realize until I climbed out the other side that I had used one or more existential verbs. Fortunately, I could use the *find* function of the word processor; the software would search through my document, looking for places where I had employed the words:

 am
 is

---

[20] I guess it depends on your definition of the word *is*. . . .

are
was
were
be
been
being
become

Every time the program halted at one of the offending conjugations, I looked at the sentence to see if I could find another way of saying the same thing. Sometimes the thought I wanted to express resisted all translation—but more often, I found that recasting the thought to omit the unwanted term would clarify it as well.

E-Prime compels the writer to look for *other* ways of saying things, instead of the immediate and easy construction. I found myself using the thesaurus function of the software a lot—it became my best friend. As an interesting and unintended side effect, my writing vocabulary expanded steadily. Indeed, the effort affected every part of my writing.

I recommend that any seriously committed writer attempt the exercise of writing in E-Prime. At the same time, I will freely acknowledge the difficulty of the task.

Eliminating the verb of static existence makes it impossible for the author to assign arbitrary qualities to things. It keeps the writer from immobilizing moments in time. He or she can no longer use language to create those specific lies of meaning, and must instead work in a more dynamic world in which things occur because someone or something makes them occur—a world in which things change with the observer.[21]

---

[21] In case you hadn't already noticed, I wrote this entire section in E-Prime.

Find Another Way

Leave the easy jobs for others.
Take the hard jobs for yourself.

The exercises with E-Prime confirmed the lesson I had previously learned with metric prose—*any* trick of style or technique will force you to find different ways to construct sentences. It will kick you out of the comfort zone of what you know into the *discomfort zone* of what you don't know—into the realm where true learning occurs.

Sometimes the word you want to use won't fit the rhythm. Sometimes the sentence construction won't work. You have to find another way of saying what you want to say. Sometimes, when you step outside the boundaries, you find a *better* way of saying it. Sometimes, you find that your original intention was insufficient to your goals. And sometimes, you stumble into whole tangents of invention that enrich your original purpose.

If your word processor has a thesaurus function, *use it.* In Microsoft Word for Windows, put the cursor on the word and hit Shift + F7. This will bring up a window that shows you alternate words. Take a moment to consider the meanings, and see if any of the alternates provide more accuracy.

If you don't have a dictionary installed on your computer, go get one *now.* My current favorite is the *American Heritage Dictionary of the English Language*, third edition, which also pronounces words. If you really want overkill, go for the CD-ROM edition of the *Oxford English*

Dictionary (which isn't a dictionary as much as it's a career.)

You have words in your vocabulary that you use unconsciously. The more unconscious words you have, the less accurately you can write. As you type, as you construct sentences, you will start to recognize that some words seem vague or uncertain to you—at such moments, you should immediately bring up your dictionary and take a moment to give yourself precision.

Literacy is your credential. You cannot afford to write unconsciously and clumsily. The more accurate your distinctions, the more accurate your thinking. The more distinctions you have, the more detailed your view of the world in which you live—and the more accurate your grasp of the controls.

Taking a moment to look for *another* way to phrase a thought gives you access to your *source*. Why? Because in such moments, you control the language, not the other way around. You become the master of possibility.

As you look for other ways to convey a concept, you will find yourself looking more accurately at your intentions, at what you want to express. This exercise wakes you up at the keyboard. It engages you. You have to actively participate in the observation of the events of your own life—and even more importantly, you will exercise and train your natural ability to look at things with *insight*. You will gain in understanding. You might even learn to grok.

Eventually, this results in a condition we call *wisdom*. . . .

Style Redux

Language is a trap. There is no escape.

This is what wisdom is for:

Writing is making decisions, one after the other. Every moment of every story is a decision, every chapter, every page, every paragraph—even every sentence. Every *word*. One decision after another: This word instead of that, this thought instead of that, this image instead of that—and decision-making is one of the most exhausting of all human activities, no matter how good at it you are.

The essential dilemma of the keyboard is the choice between effectiveness and elegance. Clarity requires that most of your sentences be simple and straightforward. But storytelling also requires vivid imagery and character and that requires a distinctive voice to evoke that imagery.

Your choice of style will be your most critical decision.

For instance, you want to say *the dragon was big*, but you also want to say it in a way that conveys the size of the beast: *The dragon loomed over the knight.* But you also want to say it in a way that evokes the lyricism and the romance of a classic myth: *Firestorm roared and Firestorm thundered; the mountains echoed and the valley shook—and the flames came rolling down.*

Not too bad, but—style represents a trap.

Why?

Because in the quest for style, a writer can end up forgetting meaning.

When you try to become beautiful, you forget who you

really are. You lose perspective. You tweak your eyebrows, curl your lashes, accentuate your cheekbones, powder your jawline. . . . You end up with too much makeup on, the lighting is wrong anyway, and you don't notice there's a piece of toilet paper stuck to your shoe. *You get pretentious.* You produce sentences that are labored, overwrought, and unsuitable for reading aloud without someone in the back tittering in embarrassment.

Nevertheless, despite the obvious danger of becoming self-parody, writers still lust after moments of perfect eloquence. It is the occupational hazard of storytelling. Sentence after sentence, you will find yourself chasing the elegant phrase like a lawyer after a loophole.

It is a mistake.

When you focus on the language instead of on the thought you want to convey, you are putting your attention in the wrong place.

The single most important lesson of effective communication is this: Focus on clarity. Concentrate on precision. Don't worry about constructing beautiful sentences. Beauty comes from meaning, not language. Accuracy is the most effective style of all.

Of course, you won't really understand this until after you've written your first million words—until *after* you've discovered this for yourself. You have to make a lot of mistakes, so you can recognize them when you make them the second, third, fourth, and twentieth time.

But even armed with this foreknowledge, and no matter how experienced you become, you will never lose that lust for the perfect phrase. And sooner or later, you *will* have to come to terms with your own quest for style.

In effect, your style is the voice of your story.

In practice, any style is a collection of tricks and techniques used to create a specific effect. Learn your tools well and you can create the voices you need.

The ultimate skill of the effective stylist is to remember that style is only voice, not content. Style is the pretense you put on for each and every story—and who you pretend to be is who you become.

Who's on First?

"I don't give a damn!"
"Oh, that's our shortstop!"

The question of person perplexes many writers. You are not alone.

Should you tell the story from the hero's point of view? If you do that, you can get inside the character's head; the hero's thoughts then become the narrative.

> Regulations specified two hours a day in the centrifuge to keep up bone strength and muscle tone. I enjoy the time in pseudogravity. Nobody bothers me. I can do my laps around the circle and let my mind go blank, just letting my feet slap-slap against the rubber decking. One-third gee is perfect for jogging. You bounce along in almost slow motion; it's a kind of exercise not possible on Earth; the only dirtside experience that even comes close is aerobics in a swimming pool, but that's a lousy substitute.

Speaking with the voice of the character allows the author to comment on the action as it unfolds. This lets the author provide strong emotional cues. It also becomes easier to reveal the character's background, because the character can freely reference events in his or her past, thus providing an enormous amount of exposition in a very short time.

I didn't like her attitude. I think it was her expression, all puckered and aloof. She reminded me of she-who-shall-not-be-named. The one who got me kicked out of school back home on Earth. It wasn't my fault though. She was telling everybody lies about my mom—so one day I just came right out and asked her if her sex change had cost so much that she couldn't afford tits . . . from the podium during the debate finals. She shrieked and ran from the stage. It was worth it. Dad was furious with me; I wasn't supposed to peek through his files; but I was angry. Anyway, that's who she reminded me of. She had the same frizzy green hair too—

But if you go to first person, you also accept some very severe restrictions. Once you climb inside that character's head, you can't get out again. You can only show what that character experiences. You can only tell what that character knows. You can't tell anything else. You can't crosscut, you can't follow any other characters, so you can't tell multi-threaded stories.

I've seen occasional attempts at this trick, where an author switches back and forth between the points of view of several different characters—and rarely successfully. To my mind, Theodore Sturgeon was the only writer who ever pulled it off well—in his last novel, *Godbody*. Why did Sturgeon succeed? Because he was skilled enough to write each character's narration in a different voice and rhythm. If the narrative voices aren't distinct, the reader can't be sure who's actually speaking.

You could try second person, but I've only seen one published story that was ever written in second person, and that was written by Arthur C. Clarke. And even he had trouble making it work.

I think there *might* be one way to tell a successful story in second person:

> Before you do anything else, read this all the way through. No, it won't help you remember, but it'll help you start over *today*.
>
> You see, there's this thing in your brain that eats your memories, so you have to start every day all over again. That's why you wrote this book for yourself. Don't lose it. This is all the memory you have.
>
> Start with this. Your name is Daniel Greep. You've been trying to find your past since January of 2012. Whatever you've learned, you've written down in this notebook. And whatever ideas you've had about where to look next, you've written those down in here too.
>
> *
>
> You don't want to go back to the office on Fifth. They'll call the police on you. It's Mrs. Tringle you have to watch out for. She might be one of *them*. Here's what happened last time you went—

That *could* work. But unless you have a brilliant story to tell, one that requires that specific approach, you're much more likely to end up with an interesting and unsalable disaster. Second person is generally a writing stunt. It calls too much attention to itself and gets in the way of the reader simply enjoying the story.

Most writers find third person the most flexible form. You can still peek inside a character's head, but the narrative point of view remains detached from any specific character. This allows the writer to crosscut between events all over the universe, with no more strain than: "Meanwhile, in another part of the galaxy. . . ."

It also presents an easier way to evoke nonhuman characters:

The drelgor flowed up the slope hungrily. It had not fed yet, and it dared not estivate until it had refilled its food sac. If its young hatched during this next long darkening, they would awake hungry. Without food to sustain them, they would grow frantic, they would eat the flesh of the parent. And then all would die. No, the drelgor needed prey.

It flowed over the crest of the ridge and paused long enough to let its eyes refocus in the actinic blue-white glare of the sun. The shadows stretched long before it, but something *strange* glinted on the land below. Unafraid—what did a drelgor have to fear?—it flowed curiously down the slope.

*

Inside the ship, Max Agg belched and scratched himself. Nothing on this godforsaken planet but rocks and wind and human beings studying rocks and wind. Oh, the sensors said that there was life here, but so far all they'd found were a few primitive things like jellyfish and bugs and seaweed. This expedition was going to be a bust. No bonus here.

*

Rrrlll waved her cilia in a pattern of yellow and infra-red, calling her life-partners closer. *I see something interesting.* She pointed at the broken land below. *Something has collated a metal penis. It glows below red. It must have fire within.* And then, she waved in even greater excitement. *The interest increases! A hungering bloat approaches—*

Which voice should you use? Try both. Then choose the one that feels most comfortable to you. You will probably find that some stories lend themselves better to first person, and some lend themselves better to third. Let the voice suit the story.

Tense

I thought, I think, I will think. . . .

Traditionally, stories are told in past tense. The author is relating events that have already occurred and are complete.

> As the ship rocked slowly back and forth, Max stared into the display. As near as he could tell, the ship was inside a giant green booger. He knew that he had to do something, but if the aft thrusters were plugged with goo, the whole ship could explode. He cursed with rage.

Occasionally, an author will attempt a work in present tense. This creates a sense of immediacy, as if the action occurs simultaneous with reader's attention.

> He grabs the ladder and slides down to the lower deck. While the ship rocks around him, he struggles into his suit—he staggers and bangs against the bulkhead; he utters a curse against the universe. His helmet still hangs in the fitting bay; he pulls it down over his head and clamps it into place. Not waiting for the final checks to complete, he grabs his volatizer from the weapons rack and rushes for the air lock. Somewhere in the middle of that giant booger, there has to be a brain—

If you want to write for motion pictures or television, you will have to learn present tense; it is the required form for story treatments, outlines, and scripts. This is because the essential language of film and video is present tense— the story happens in the moment of *now*. So the film outline or script also has to happen in the *now*. Present tense accomplishes that.

> EXT. THE SHIP. As the drelgor continues to rock . . .

> INT. THE AIR LOCK. Angry now, Max slaps the access panel. The outer hatch slides open! The blubbery mass of the drelgor bulges IN THROUGH THE HATCH!

> SPFX: MAX FIRES THE VOLATIZER. The crackling beam hits the wet gooey flesh of the beast. IT RECOILS!

> EXT. THE SHIP. The drelgor CONVULSES. It shudders and writhes, but does not release its hold.

> INT. THE AIR LOCK. Max is thrown violently from side to side.

> SPFX: He FIRES again! But this time—

For short stories and novels, however, you should exercise restraint. *Enormous* restraint.

Present tense is extremely effective for creating a sense of immediacy. It's a very visual style, and it helps the story play like a movie in the reader's imagination. A skilled stylist can segue into present tense so smoothly the reader will never notice. (The best example of this is the brilliant climax of Norman Spinrad's classic novel, *Bug Jack Barron*. Worth seeking out. Also look for his story "Carcinoma Angels," first published in Harlan Ellison's *Dangerous Visions* anthology, and *"Weed of Time"*, first published in Anne McCaffrey's *Alchemy and Academe* anthology.)

Present tense is a useful tactic for stepping away from the rest of your narrative. It makes each moment more intense, but many readers find it a disconcerting break in style. It tends to call attention to itself, and it often feels like a stunt. It is inappropriate for traditional forms of storytelling, especially fantasy. If you cannot make a compelling case for using present tense for your narrative style, *don't* do it.

There's one other tense you might want to be aware of. That's future tense. For obvious reasons, it is practically *impossible* to tell a story in future tense:

> Max will fail, of course. He has no chance against a creature that has no central brain structure. He will discover the hard way that drelgors are amorphous carnivores—like a giant stomach turned inside out.
>
> Max will fall backward into the interior of the ship; hull security will be breached—he'll scramble downward to the engineering level and grab the fire extinguisher. Maybe he'll be able to freeze the creature with liquid CO_2.
>
> But he won't have enough! And the drelgor will come bulging down through the open hatch, hungry and slobbering, dripping and drooling with anticipation. The smell will be horrible.

Can you imagine trying to read a story like that? Let alone write one? The inherent flaw in future tense is that it tells you this *hasn't* happened yet. It implies that there's a choice. The entire manuscript will scream for a well-placed *if*.

While future tense is useful for discussing and even predicting the future, if you want to tell a story that actually occurs in the future, you have to tell it as if you are a contemporary observer in and of that time. Future tense doesn't work because it doesn't let you write from the inside.

Pronouns

Characters are he, she, or it.
Those are the choices. Why?

Readers are used to seeing characters described as he or she. This is a cultural bias. We don't have pronouns for neuters or transgendered or hermaphroditic people because those conditions don't occur often enough for our language to require the specific distinction.

People whose identity is not suitably described as *he* or *she* find no acknowledgment of their state in the language; there is no accommodation. The language shoehorns their identities into existing and often inappropriate categories. It turns out that there are quite a few folks who believe that *he* and *she* are inappropriate descriptors—and the pronoun *it* is offensive and dehumanizing. (Every so often, someone tries to invent a new pronoun, one that is gender neutral. Most of the experiments I've seen have seemed artificial and uncomfortable. None of them have achieved general usage.)

Science fiction and fantasy writers bump up against the problem every time they deal with the issue of gender. *He* and *she* are insufficient for discussing the spectrum of human behavior. *He* and *she* represent a binary, on/off, yes/no, male/female, yang/yin, either-or realm of sexual identity. There's no in-between in that symbol set. They do not allow for the identification of gay, lesbian, bisexual, transgendered, neuter, hermaphroditic, celibate, or disinterested. In effect, the words function as a flat black-and-white representation of a multicolored stereo landscape.

We cannot expect that alien races will have two sexes. What if they only have one? What if they have three or seven? What if they have none at all? What if they choose their sex at puberty? What if they cycle through different sexual identities as they grow? What kind of language can you use to describe such identities? You can't even explore the psychology of such a species without an appropriate language.

Of course, if you never choose to write about such societies, you'll never have to confront this problem—but if you do take on the challenge, you will have to solve the problem. You will find that the English language does not lend itself to the consideration of gender identities outside the binary paradigm. Whatever solution you create, it will likely feel artificial and labored.

In some situations, the best solution is to identify your character as an *it*. Perhaps you're writing about a sentient machine, a robot, or an alien. Identifying it as *he* or *she* automatically conveys a whole set of cultural assumptions, whereas *it* reminds the reader, albeit subtly, that the character cannot be classified by a binary paradigm of gender. (In *The Moon Is a Harsh Mistress*, Robert A. Heinlein wrote about a sentient computer called "Mike." Mike was male in his relations with the hero and female in her relations with the heroine.)

Our language fosters a cultural prejudice that gender can exist only as male/female and everything else is different—as in *alien* and *wrong*. But science fiction *and* fantasy include a mandate to reexamine existing notions of the way things are. The whole point of speculative fiction is to explore other possibilities, and gender is one of the great unexplored continents of literature.

Aliens will *not* have gender as we do. Nor will elemental

entities like demons. If you bring to life a mountain, a black hole, the wind, an automobile, a toaster—it need not necessarily have a gender either. In such cases, you would certainly want to use *it*. By using *it* instead of *he* or *she*, you prevent the reader from assigning those qualities to the robot, the alien, the demon, or the toaster. *It* makes the entity a little more alien and mysterious.

There are other pronoun tricks you can use as well. For instance, you can challenge the existing cultural assumptions of the reader by popping in the unexpected pronoun. This is the kind of surprise that can enhance your story with a detail that sticks in the reader's mind:

> Balfug the guard felt exhausted and resentful. High up here, on the cold drafty battlements, everything was smothered under fog. The night closed in like a wet woolen blanket—there was nothing to see, nothing to hear. This was nasty and unnecessary duty, and Balfug wanted nothing more than to return to the warm stoves of the north tower, but not while the lieutenants were drinking and entertaining themselves with their boys. Balfug spat and uttered a disdainful curse; she hated this duty—

In a novel called *Moonstar Odyssey*, I postulated a world where everyone chooses their gender at puberty. This suggested to me that the people of this world might use a single pronoun for both sexes, so I used *she* for every character in the book, even the males. It was not always obvious which characters were male or female until they identified themselves as such, and this forced the readers to stop using gender identity as a way of defining the characters in their minds. Some readers were disconcerted by the trick, but it helped create a specific mood for the world.

I tried a different trick in a project called *Sea of Grass*. The protagonist-narrator is a ten-year-old named Kaer. I started writing thinking Kaer was a male, then a few pages in realized it might be better if Kaer was a female—and then I stopped and wondered if it was necessary to identify Kaer's gender at all. What if I didn't? How would it affect the perception of the character? How would it affect the character's relationships with everyone else in the story? What would it imply about this particular world?

I didn't know if that would work, but it was worth a try; so whenever I started to write a sentence where *he* or *she* might be necessary, I substituted another phrasing:

"Ask Kaer," Lorrin said. "The child will know."

Is it possible to write a gender-neutral character in a story? With the text not establishing Kaer's gender, the reader's own perceptions of Kaer might fill in the gap. And that might be the lesson here—that as human beings, we *cannot* have identity without gender being a crucial determinant.

As you write, you may discover or invent other pronoun tricks of your own. These will be useful to you to the extent they allow you to break outside this culture's paradigm of *he* and *she*.

800 Words

*Say what you have to say. Say it three times.
The first time so they will hear it, the second
time so they will REALLY hear it, and the third
time so they will get it. Then get off the stage.*

A.E. Van Vogt, one of the classic science fiction writers of
the golden age of science fiction, had his own formula for
storytelling. He introduced a new idea every 800 words—
every four pages. The idea could be a new place or a new
machine or a new way of thinking, but every 800 words,
he reinvented your expectations.

This had the effect of giving his stories a breathless pace;
his heroes moved from one fantastic moment to the next,
and the reader never had a chance to get impatient or bored.

Much of Van Vogt's work was written for *Astounding
Science Fiction*, edited by John W. Campbell. Although
Astounding had its roots in the pulp-fiction magazines of
the twenties and thirties, by the mid-forties, it was already
establishing itself as something *more*. Under Campbell's
early guidance, and later under the hands of other writer-
editors, like H.L. Gold and Frederik Pohl at *Galaxy Science
Fiction*, and Anthony Boucher at *The Magazine of Fantasy
and Science Fiction* the genre began to mature toward a
more serious contemplation of ideas and philosophy.

A.E. Van Vogt ("Van" to his friends and colleagues) was
one of those authors who was continually exploring the
outer fringes. In the late forties, he was impressed by *Science and Sanity: An Introduction to Non-Aristotelian Sys-*

tems and General Semantics by Alfred Korzybski. Van Vogt used these theories in *The World of Null-A*, about a world that had moved beyond Aristotelian logic. The four-part serial started in the August 1945 issue of *Astounding Science Fiction*, and became an instant classic. Van Vogt continued his research into alternate ways of thinking and for a time during the fifties, was actively involved with *Dianetics*, L. Ron Hubbard's precursor to Scientology. He died from complications of pneumonia in January of 2000.

What makes Van Vogt interesting is not just his body of work—much of which is suffused with a dreamlike quality unmatched by any other writer of his generation—but his willingness to move beyond the usual limits of pulp fiction. Many of his best stories were written from the unconscious side of his mind. To many readers, Van Vogt's stories were puzzling, even confusing. But he had an enormous following among science fiction fans because of the inventiveness of his work.

Half a century later, Van Vogt's work endures. Why? Because of his simple trick of taking the reader to a new place, every 800 words. Try it and see if it works for you.

Dialogue, Part I

Eavesdrop. Don't get caught.

"Of all the different challenges in storytelling, I like doing dialogue best," the instructor said to the class.

"Oh yeah? Why?" asked the skeptical student.

"Because dialogue provides the most direct form of interaction with a person. It reveals exactly who the characters are by what they say and the way they speak."

The student considered the idea. "I guess so. That sorta makes sense."

The instructor leaned forward on the desk. "Your mistake lies in thinking that dialogue must be conversation. It *isn't*. It only *looks* like it. Look, when you write dialogue, you only want to create the *illusion* of conversation while presenting the necessary interaction in as few lines as possible."

The student frowned, still trying to wrap his head around the thought.

The instructor said, "Here, try this experiment. Eavesdrop on other people's conversations. Go to a restaurant and listen to the people at the table behind you. Listen to the way they speak to each other."

"I've done that," said the student. "I listen in all the time."

"And?" prompted the instructor. "What have you noticed?"

"Most conversations are *really* boring."

"Do you know why?"

The student shook his head.

"People don't edit their conversations for dramatic impact—they make it up as they go. So they fumble their way, unrehearsed, from one moment to the next. The average interaction takes twenty minutes to resolve. The audience doesn't have that much patience. You have to trim the conversation down to the most important points. Create the flavor of a much deeper discussion, but get to the punch line as fast as you can. If the dialogue goes on for more than three pages, you've taken too long."

"Oh," said the student.

Dialogue, Part II

"Shut up!" he explained.

"I've got a shipload of pfingle eggs, and no pilot," Tranny growled.

"Too bad," Velga sniffed. "I'm not interested in the commission."

"You can't afford to have an attitude," he barked.

"Neither can you!" she snorted.

"All right," Tranny muttered. "I'll pay you a percentage."

"Still not interested," Velga sang.

"What is it you want?!!" he yelled.

"An apology!" she shouted.

"For what?!!" he demanded.

"For your bad manners!!" she snapped.

"I saved your life!" he insisted.

"You saved your investment!" she retorted.

"This is blackmail," he whined.

"This is bargaining," she whispered.

"Oh, the hell with it. I apologize," he said.

I'll bet you were really grateful for that *said*, weren't you? What *else* was wrong with that exchange? Try this instead:

Tranny looked unhappy. "Can I sit down?"

Velga shrugged. "The chair is empty."

Tranny sat. "Can I buy you a beer?"

"I've already got a beer." Velga held up her glass; the beer looked greener than usual in the blue light of the bar. "What do you want?"

"I've got a shipload of pfingle eggs, and no pilot."

"Too bad," Velga sniffed. "I'm not interested in the commission."

"I heard you need work. You can't afford to be choosy."

"Considering you have a cargo of pfingle eggs, neither can you." She sipped at her beer. It had gone bitter. She made a face and put the glass back down on the table.

Tranny misinterpreted her expression. He made a noise like a broken volatizer valve. But he didn't dare say what he was obviously thinking. "I'm desperate," he admitted. "I'll pay you a percentage."

"Still not interested."

"What do you want?" he asked, frustrated.

"An apology would be nice."

"An apology?" Tranny was incredulous. "I saved your life!"

"You saved your investment," she said impassively.

"This is blackmail."

"This is *bargaining*."

"The hell you say!"

"You need a pilot?"

Tranny made as if to stand up. But he didn't. He sank back into his chair, defeated. "Oh, all right. I apologize," he said.

"You didn't mean that," she accused.

"It's as good as you're going to get, so you might as well accept it."

Effective dialogue needs descriptive action interspersed throughout. This gives detail and context. If you intend to create the illusion of a real conversation, then you need to create all the business that attends a real conversation. Real people eat and drink, they smoke and cough, they fold their arms, they cross their legs, they scratch themselves, they readjust their positions on the couch, they shrug, they sink back in their chairs, they pause, they look away, they hesitate, they consider their next words carefully, they look uncomfortable, they nod thoughtfully, they smile through their teeth, they pretend to understand, and sometimes they even *listen*.

If you want to create the sense that these are real people talking, then you need to suggest some of the physical events that are occurring as they talk. If dialogue is the best way to reveal a character, then the second-best way is through the description that accompanies dialogue.

Many writers find dialogue one of the most enjoyable parts of storytelling, because they get to spend quality time with their characters. Dialogue is where the real acting happens—and most important, it is where the real transformations occur.

Discipline

A writer is two kinds of machine.
He is a perpetual notion machine.
He is a perpetual emotion machine.

In addition to talking about structure, Irwin R. Blacker also taught writing discipline.

If you write whenever you feel like it, you will have pages. If you write every day, you will have a book. You have to finish what you start, so don't start anything unless you have a profound commitment to finishing it.

Blacker's technique was very simple. He'd set himself a target every day. Eight pages, ten pages, whatever. He'd sit down at the typewriter—yes, we're talking a long, long time ago—and he wouldn't get up again until he'd written the eight or ten or twelve pages he'd committed to write. A typewritten page will have approximately 200–250 words, depending on how you set your margins and what size type you use, 10 or 12 point. So a commitment to ten pages represented 2,000–2,500 words.

When I wrote my first novel, I applied the same discipline. I would sit down at my typewriter in the morning and not get up until I had written a complete chapter—*a chapter I was satisfied with*—then I was free to take the rest of the day off. Usually, I was done by midafternoon. I would work five or six days a week. I finished my first and second novels in the space of three months. In the next three months, I wrote my third novel and fourteen chapters of a fourth.

Discipline works.

Of course, it helps if you live in New York. Why? Because then you can open your window in the morning and listen to the city growl at you: *"If you don't write today, I will kill you. I will crush you, I will grind your bones, I will drink your blood and destroy you. Oh, maybe not today, and maybe not tomorrow—but if you don't write today, in a month you'll be broke . . . and then I'll get you!"* There are few better incentives than the threat of starvation. (Fear is almost as good as rage to fuel your writing engine.)

Today, more than ever, I remain a firm believer in a strict writing discipline. Instead of counting pages, though, I count words. I set myself a target of 1,000–3,000 words a day, depending on the type of project I'm writing.

To monitor my progress, I use a spreadsheet that I designed myself during the course of writing several books. It tracks my progress toward my goal and measures my effectiveness.

At the end of every writing session, I tell the word processing program to count the number of words in the file. I enter the number into the spreadsheet as that day's result. The spreadsheet compares that result with the previous day's result, then reports how many words I've written today and what percentage of my target I've achieved. It even tells me approximately how many days left until the book is finished.

This becomes a way that I can compete with myself. I'm always aiming for my personal best: *Yesterday, I did 112 percent of my daily target. Today I'll go for 125 percent.*

I've occasionally shared this system with other folks who write—and in all candor, some of them have been horrified. The idea that writing can be quantified, disciplined, and ultimately produced by quota, like carving slices off a sausage offends their artistic sensibilities. What about passion? What about inspiration? What about Art (with a capital A)?

What about it?

The fact is that more great books have been written by folks with mediocre ability and an unquenchable discipline than have ever been written by talented geniuses with no discipline.

In my life, I have been lucky enough to meet several people of such enormous talent that I was breathless with jealousy. But you've never heard of them. Why? They didn't finish what they started.

If you don't finish it, you can't publish it. And if you don't publish, you aren't a writer; you're a dilettante.

Once, in a writing workshop I was conducting at a convention, one "student" patiently explained that before she started writing, she was going to read all the best books on writing and take all the best courses. She wasn't going to write her book until she could make it perfect. I suppose she actually believed that.

My response wasn't kind—but it was useful. I told her flat out that what she had just said was her excuse for *not* writing.

Real writers *write*.

You learn by doing.

Apply the seat of the pants to the seat of the chair and don't get up until you have written at least 1,000 words of something. Anything.

When Ray Bradbury was first starting out, he set himself the goal of writing one short story a week. He said, "It's impossible to write fifty-two bad short stories in a year." (Of course, it helps if you're Ray Bradbury. I was afraid to try that discipline. I was afraid I'd prove him wrong.)

You don't learn how to swim by reading a book about swimming, and you don't learn how to dance by reading a book about dancing. Those things are coaching, not teaching. And you don't learn how to write by reading a book about writing. *This book is coaching.*

All that stuff about passion and inspiration and art— yeah, that's important. That's *always* the goal. But the way you get there is through discipline. Remember the old joke about the guy who asks for directions in New York City:

"How do you get to Carnegie Hall?"
"Practice, buddy. Practice."

That's how you get *anywhere.*

If you want to be a great piano player, you practice and you practice and you practice, every day of your life; you play the piano eight hours a day. If you want to be a great swimmer, you have to get in the pool and swim a hundred laps a day. If you want to run the marathon, you have to run a mile, two miles, three miles a day.

You train by *doing.*

And you have to enjoy the *doing.* (If you don't enjoy the process, you probably shouldn't write.)

After you have trained yourself, *after* you have built up your writing muscles, *after* you have learned how to apply the hard lessons you have learned, then you will find that you have a profound set of skills to put at the service of your passion.

Discipline not only serves success—it *deserves* success.

The First Million Words

Relax. . . .

Your first million words are for practice.

They don't count. Remember that.

You will practice writing stories. You will practice writing novels. You will practice and practice and practice. It doesn't count.

You will practice sending your stories out. Don't be afraid—it doesn't count. You will practice receiving rejection slips. Remember, they don't count either. If some editor somewhere is so desperate for something to publish that he accidentally makes the mistake of buying one of your practice stories, don't think it means anything; it doesn't. It's still practice. Go to the bank and practice cashing the check.

If you haven't written a million words—that's approximately ten novels—you're still practicing.

If you accidentally sell a novel and it gets published, it's still practice. And if you get invited to make a guest appearance on Oprah or Rosie, it's still practice. And if you win the National Book Award or the Hugo or the Nebula, then practice accepting the award. Get up, say thank you, and sit down again quickly. (Anything else will be embarrassing.)

Don't forget. If you haven't written a million words, it's all practice.

After you've written a million words, *then* you can take yourself seriously.

Be Specific

Here's the lesson I learned from D.C. Fontana.

Dorothy C. Fontana is one of the finest television writers in Hollywood. She was the story editor of *Star Trek* (the original series), associate producer of the animated *Star Trek* series, and a producer on *Star Trek: The Next Generation*. She has also written scripts for *Logan's Run*, *The Waltons*, *Streets of San Francisco*, *Lonesome Dove*, *Land of the Lost*, *Babylon 5*, and many other television shows.

I met her shortly after I sold my first script to *Star Trek*. She took me aside to help me understand script format. She pointed to a line I wrote:

Kirk reacts.

"How does he react?" she asked. "Bill's a good actor, and I'm sure he'll figure out what to do. But when a writer puts down 'Kirk reacts' and doesn't say how, then maybe the writer isn't really sure *how* Kirk reacts. You have to be specific."

So on the next draft, I wrote:

Kirk reacts sharply.

She caught me on it again. "Nope. That's a cheat. Try again."

Kirk reacts with annoyance.
Kirk reacts with horror.

Kirk reacts with amusement.
Kirk looks unhappy.
Kirk scowls in frustration.

She was right.

I learned the lesson *again*, the first time I submitted a story to Harlan Ellison for his second *Dangerous Visions* anthology.

A little history first: During the sixties and well into the seventies, science fiction reinvented itself at least six times over. Authors wanted to move beyond the older structures and restrictions; they wanted to explore beyond the boundaries of convention.

If the fifties had been the first golden age of science fiction, then the sixties were the second golden age. Phillip Jose Farmer wrote *The Lovers*, about a love affair between a man and an alien woman. Theodore Sturgeon wrote "A World Well Lost," one of the very first stories to acknowledge the emotional component of a homosexual relationship. Walter M. Miller Jr. published *A Canticle for Leibowitz*, about a second religious dark age after a catastrophic meltdown of civilization. Robert A. Heinlein, long considered the "dean" of science fiction, released his most startling and controversial novel, *Stranger in a Strange Land*, in which a man raised by Martians brings a new way of thinking to Earth—the book explores sex, religion, general semantics, politics, merchandising, bigotry, evolution, and half a dozen other heavyweight themes along the way. Frank Herbert published *Dune*, a complex epic that touched on mysticism, drugs, religion, revolution, and history. These and other stories were a far cry from *The War of the Worlds* and *From the Earth to the Moon*.

At the same time, the field began to experience an influx of women writers. Kate Wilhelm, Anne McCaffrey, Judith

Merrill, Zenna Henderson, Marion Zimmer Bradley, Joanna Russ, and Ursula K. LeGuin quickly became familiar names. They brought a different set of perspectives to the genre, and engendered (pun intended) a long-overdue and very healthy reassessment of science fiction's approach to sex and gender—and after that, everything else as well.

But many of the existing science fiction magazines and anthologies didn't know how to assimilate the changes that were taking place in the field. A lot of these stories went too far beyond existing editorial policies. Perhaps the most astonishing voice in the field during those days was Harlan Ellison, who wrote stories of such profound pain and passion that they stick in your mind like a fish-bone caught in your throat—stories like "Shattered Like a Glass Goblin," "Pretty Maggie Moneyeyes," "The Deathbird," "I Have No Mouth, and I Must Scream," and my personal favorite, " 'Repent, Harlequin!' Said the Ticktockman."

Chafing at what he perceived as arbitrary and foolish restrictions, Ellison assembled a new kind of anthology. *Dangerous Visions* was the place for all those stories that couldn't be published anywhere else, because of subject matter or style or editorial prejudice, stories that were "dangerous" to the status quo. From the git-go, the anthology was regarded as the most prestigious collection of authors and stories ever assembled in science fiction.

The first book was so successful that Ellison began collecting stories for a second one, *Again, Dangerous Visions*. That was when I showed up on his doorstep, clutching my precious manuscript in my hand.

It was one of the most horrifying experiences in my life. And one of the best.

Uncle Harlan went through that manuscript line by line and demonstrated in excruciating detail why my first-and-worst writing instructor had been absolutely right in his assessment of my ability. I really *couldn't* write.

I could put down sentences on paper, and they sort of looked like a story, but in truth, most of what I had written wasn't much better than the work of a chimpanzee fumbling at a keyboard. My work was amateur and primitive—I had never been properly trained. High school English wasn't enough; the college courses in creative writing and journalism were insufficient. The essential foundation of writing lies in the skill of constructing an insightful sentence—and I'd never been exposed to that discussion, not in six years of higher education. (And not from lack of trying either.)

As a writer, I was functionally illiterate. I was putting down words without any thought behind them.

This was the trap of the "new wave" of experimental fiction. All that freedom that writers craved—it also served as license. (I have said elsewhere, I have even put it into the mouths of my characters, that "freedom is *not* license, it is *responsibility*." But at that point in time, I hadn't yet learned the lesson myself.)

In the breakaway from traditional form, what had also occurred was a disinheritance of the foundations of story-telling structure. Much of this experimentation was necessary, creating an important expansion of the range of ideas and treatments available to authors, yet it also gave comfort to the idea that traditional forms were worthless and should be discarded. The result, for a while, was a nihilistic abandonment of story.

Fortunately, this trend didn't last long—

While Ellison often gets blamed for some of the worst excesses of the period, the truth is that he was one of the most rigorous and demanding of editors. For Ellison, it isn't enough to be passionate about what you write—you also have to be eloquent. You have to sparkle.

After about three pages of Uncle Harlan's line-by-line dissection of *Men Without Faces* (a story which I have long since burned in embarrassment), I began to get a glimpse of what I had been missing.

You have to know what you want to say.

If you have no clear goal, then you're just fumbling around, smearing paint on the canvas, pounding randomly on the piano keys, and throwing yourself about on the stage in semblance of performance. If you don't really know what you're evoking, then all the excesses of style and form and tense and person will not disguise it.

The lesson was *insight.*

You have to look inside yourself and accurately identify the moment.

And then you have to report it clearly.

Clearly!

Why Write?

Life is not a rehearsal.

When I started teaching writing, one of the questions I began asking my students was this: *Why write?*

Over the years, I heard many different answers.

Theodore Sturgeon used to say, "Because it's easier than *not* writing." And while that's a pretty good answer, it's too clever by half. It's an answer that I suspect can only be understood by someone who writes regularly. Writers nod when they hear it, but people who do not write just crinkle their brows in puzzlement.

Samuel R. Delaney once said, "Because there are stories I want to read and I can't find them in the library, so I have to write them myself." When I heard him say that, it *resonated.* Yes! All the places I want to go, all the things I want to see, all the adventures I want to have—if no one else will write those books, then I have to.

But even that answer wasn't enough. Both of those answers are selfish in that the attention is on the writer, not on the story, not on the reader.

A story is an act of communication.

If no one reads it, it doesn't exist, the communication *doesn't* happen.

And if it does happen—then what is it you *want* to have happen?

This was the lesson I discovered for myself:

What I do in the world has an effect on the people around me. I am responsible for the effect I produce on others.

Most of what we humans do in life is communication.

We talk, we write, we send e-mails, we leave voice messages; we read newspapers, magazines, books; we listen to the radio, we watch television, we log onto the Internet. We transmit and receive ideas, thoughts, feelings, opinions, and emotions. Beyond that, we sing songs, we paint pictures, we play music, we dance to communicate things that can't quite be codified by words.

Look into any relationship and you will find that the essential nature of the relationship *is* communication. To the extent that the communication works, the relationship works.

The better our communications, the better our lives work. Investigate any problem and you will find at its core a failure to communicate clearly. Investigate any success and you will find clear and accurate communication among the participants.

As a human being, you make a difference. Simply by existing, simply by being in the room, you *make a difference.*

The question that I had to ask myself was this—what kind of difference do I want to make?

That was the most important lesson.

And now I pass it on to you. Before you sit down at your keyboard, ask yourself: What kind of difference do *you* want to make?

What you write has an effect on the people who read it. Words have meaning. Ideas have consequences.

Your book, your story, your script—whatever you write—that's your way of challenging the world. What do *you* want to say to the rest of your species?

Ten Pieces of Good Advice

*Good advice is worth exactly
what you paid for it.*

- You are what you pretend. Pretend big.
- Be your own biggest fan.
- Be your most ferocious critic.
- Impatience is fatal. Enjoy each moment of your story. If you don't, no one else will.
- You can't write what you don't know. If you don't know, find out.
- Show. Don't tell.
- Create expectations. Then defy them. Surprise yourself.
- Write your own story.
- Be passionate.
- Aim for the stars.
- Never eat anything larger than your lawyer.

Recommendations

Typing Tutor: *Mavis Beacon Teaches Typing*.
Screenwriting: *Scriptware*. (Windows or Macintosh).
Word Processing: *Microsoft Word for Windows*.
Software Dictionary: *American Heritage Dictionary of the English Language,* third edition.
Style Guide: *The Elements of Style*, William Strunk Jr. and E.B. White.

Index